My Mother's Girdle

Girdle

A Collection

Anne Warren Smith

Some of the essays published in this edition were first published
elsewhere. Acknowledgements appear with each piece.

These essays are based on the author's memory. They are true,
for the author, even when they are not factual. Other family
members will almost certainly have different memories.

Published by Anne Warren Smith

ISBN: 978-1507877463

CreateSpace Independent Publishing Platform
2015

First Edition

Cover illustration copyright © 2015 Jan Dymond

Interior designer Amy Beltaine

Interior illustrations and photo preparation
by Amy Beltaine and Rebecca Smith

Children's Books
by Anne Warren Smith

Blue Denim Blues

Sister in the Shadow

Turkey Monster Thanksgiving

Tails of Spring Break

Bittersweet Summer

Second-Chance Summer

See more at http://www.annewarrensmith.com

Dedicated to
all those people who trusted
me with their stories.

Contents

Prologue

The black and white photo on my desk is really a portrait of three things: my brother Jack, me as a baby, and the winged chair. Someone has propped me next to him in the chair and my chin and ears are disappearing into the neck of my stiff baby dress. He's got one foot tucked under him, a cute kid in shorts and leather shoes that tie, and he's smiling at someone, probably at Mother. It is 1938. Jack is three.

In the picture, my round, dark eyes are locked on some kind of toy Jack is holding in his lap. I'm much too small to wrestle that toy away from him, but I see he's already learned to hold things close. He's like Mother in that way. He appreciates the trappings of family roots—the clocks, the iron trivets, the old snowshoes in the basement. He'll take care of them and honor their importance.

This book began as I thought about something that had been missing from my childhood. Not knowing what it was I mourned, I chose to write about hats and girdles, salmon loaf, sterling silver, and kitchen cupboards. Do these essays hang together somehow?

My editors and I decided that with stretching and pulling we could make them all fit into a theme of growing up voiceless and finding my voice.

As I reread them I realize that there is an omission. I have never spoken of my brother's story growing up in our home. Like any two siblings we must have protected each other. I can hear him defending me from having to wear gloves to a birthday party. I can hear myself defending him from appearing in a suit jacket at the same event. I'm sure this occurred over and over. Over the years we grew apart. We grew back together during my divorce, and during our parents aging and final illnesses.

The winged chair appears now and then in my stories. By the time I was seventy, it was in storage in my nephew Erik's Minnesota pole barn along with boxes filled with things that were previously crammed into Mother's house. After seventy years, the cushion still ballooned with goose down, each front leg still ended in a polished claw and ball. I imagined that next to the chair was the footstool with its needlepointed top. Jack would have moved the chair and the footstool together; he would have stored them together.

The chair, along with the other things in the pole barn issued impossible commands to me and Jack, to my children and his children. Store us, polish us, admire us. Tell our stories. Let us fill you, and all your closets, up.

The chair came in the Thirties from a store in Glens Falls, in upstate New York. In those days, in those little upstate towns, owning a chair like this one may have signaled modest wealth. My short mother always wanted to be looked up to which explains the girdles, the heels, and her tone of voice. Possibly, it also explains why she loved cups without handles, saucers without cups, and even empty cardboard boxes. "We might need that," she'd say. "That paring knife came from Great Aunt Jette." "My grandmother quilted that." She pats a faded fabric gently into a drawer and looks up at the framed mirror above the dresser. "There's a frame just like this one in the White House."

Some mothers empower a husband or a son or a daughter through praise, attention, and support. That was not my mother's way. She had many beautiful objects, and she preferred to give her power to them.

The author in the center. Her mother (Laura Myers Warren), in the chair.
Back row: sister-in-law, dad ("Bob" Thurman Clifford Warren), brother (Jack), husband (Fred Smith).
Front Row: nephew, daughter (Rebecca), niece, daughter (Amy)

My Mother's Girdle

CALYX, A Journal of Art and Literature by Women 21.1
(Winter 2003).

There's a book on my shelf called *The History of Underclothes*.* A few years ago I ordered it from Dover Publications and gave it to my mother, who studied fashion design in college. She returned it unread. "It's nonfiction," she told me. "With that title, I expected a romance novel." I leaf through it now and I'm fascinated. The book documents Woman's quest for the "right" contours from medieval times to the 1940s. If there's a second volume, it will have to include briefs with tummy control panels, the Wonderbra, and Barbie.

On my desk is a column I clipped about a recent version of Barbie, the one Mattel is calling President Barbie. Wearing four-inch heels, carrying a briefcase, she underlines the shapely message women have received for centuries: How we look is what really matters. With her impossibly tiny waist, Barbie deserves her own chapter in *The History of Underclothes*. The column says today's average American

---

**The History of Underclothes* by C. Willett and Phyllis Cunningham (Dover Publications, Inc., 1992). All quotations are used by permission of the publisher.

girl owns eight of these stiff, "shapely" dolls. I grew up before Barbies. Not to worry. I had my mother.

Sitting cross-legged on the floor next to the bookcase, I leaf through old photos, looking for Mother in the days before I was born. In her 1932 college graduation picture, she wears a lace-trimmed dress, a single string of pearls, and perfectly plucked dark eyebrows. Her hair is brushed back in soft waves and tucked into a bun. I can't see her waist or hips, but I know what I know. She's wearing her girdle. I know this because for all the years I lived at home, I saw Mother emerge from her bedroom each morning dressed for gardening, cleaning, canning, shopping, or the garden club meeting. Always looking "dressed." Always, always, wearing her girdle.

Mother bought me white gloves and taught me how to choose a spring hat and how to sit with my knees together. She modeled the perfect housewife as she shined windows, waxed floors, and oiled furniture. When I learned the correct way to set a table, I knew I should get out the milk pitcher even for breakfast. No bottles on our table! I learned that making the clearest currant jelly could show great creativity. That *Vogue* made the most stylish patterns. That dinner parties began with Manhattans in the proper glass and finished with cream puffs on the proper plate.

Wearing her girdle, stockings, and heels, Mother never looked like anyone else's mother. I figured we had royalty in our blood. One day when I was eleven, Mother confirmed this when she opened the blue wooden trunk at the foot of her bed and pulled out my great-grandmother's green brocade wedding dress. With its skinny sleeves and tiny waist, fastened with hundreds of buttons and loops, Nonna's dress was truly fit for a princess. I put it on and regally posed for photos, twirling the matching parasol, watching the fringe fly out. *The History of Underclothes* tells me Nonna probably wore a corset under that dress. I find the following: "In the 1890s it was a girl's ambition to have, at marriage, a waist-measurement not exceeding the number of years of her age—and to marry before she was twenty-one."

I look for pictures of tiny Nonna, but instead, uncover a photo of her daughter, my grandmother, about 1905, in her own wedding dress. I study the lace that covered her neck, the filmy loose sleeves. The white dress blouses out in front, tucks in back, making her look like a poster child for swayback. Flipping pages in *The History of Underclothes*, I read words taken from *The Lady's Realm*, a fashion journal of the time: "Fashion decrees that very large hips and great splendour of figure should prevail but also superimposes a distinctly diminutive waist. A good waistline is after all very much a matter of one's corset."

When I was a child, we took the train downstate along the Hudson River once a year to visit that same Grandma on the farm in the Catskills. I remember how her eyes crinkled up with tears of happiness as we stepped off the train. I remember hugs, soft as bread dough. I gorged on sugar cookies that were stored in a pale blue glass container in Grandma's big pantry. "Of course, you may have a cookie," Grandma would say. When I reached in, my hand turned pale blue.

In unroyal fashion, Grandma wore her stockings rolled down around her ankles. Somehow I knew Mother hated that she did. I watched as Mother pinned crocheted doilies over threadbare upholstery and straightened the heaps of *Farm Journals*. In the bathroom, she blew ashes off the window sill and stacked up the ashtray, the tiny silver lighter, and the pack of Chesterfields. She shook her head at Grandma's solitaire board and the deck of cards beside the toilet. While I gorged on cookies and Grandma's praise, Mother's voice grew thin. Once she asked Grandma, "Why don't you get rid of those worn-out shoes?"

"These shoes feel good," Grandma answered. Then she and I would go out to the garden to pick a watermelon or we'd choose a wooden jigsaw puzzle from all the puzzles stacked on the attic stairs. Our visits always ended before our puzzles were finished. When we left, Grandma's face crumpled into deep wrinkles and she rubbed her eyes with the corners of her apron.

On the train going home, Mother would get out her compact and dab powder on her nose. With her finger, she'd wet down a stray eyebrow hair. And then she'd notice my gloves, no longer white. "What have you been touching?" she'd ask.

The girdle my ninety-year-old mother still wears was advertised as a "corselette" in the 1920s, in those years before she went to college. It's a breast-to-bottom elastic and satin contraption with garters. Nowadays, she has to order it from a specialty lingerie store. Today, when she puts it on, she tugs with fingers that are swollen with arthritis, first one side, then the other. She tucks in folds of soft, white skin. Finally, she pulls the straps over her shoulders, catching her breasts into the cups.

The garters, of course, have to be fastened to her stockings, since a girdle without a crotch needs stockings to hold it down. She rolls a stocking down to its foot and points her toe. The girdle doesn't let her bend far, but she lifts her knee just enough to poke her foot into the stocking and begins to unroll the nylon up her leg. By the time both stockings are fastened into the garters, she has to rest. But a few minutes later, she's at the mirror in a pretty skirt and blouse, patting her face with glycerin and rose water, dabbing on powder and lipstick. My aunts discarded their girdles forty years ago in favor of physical freedom. "They let themselves go," my mother says.

Today, the straps have dug permanent ridges into her shoulders. Her back and abdomen muscles have no strength. Her insides hurt, she says, and her doctor tells me nothing prevents her organs from sagging into each other. Her voice is strong, however, and she's full of opinions, especially about people who are not well-off. She hires these people to work for her. Her furniture still gleams, her chests still hold antique clothes and silver trays. She still uses the milk pitcher at the breakfast table.

My mother is trapped in her corselette mind. My dictionary tells me that one of the definitions of girdle is "to surround. To enclose or confine on all sides so as to bar escape or outside communication." Mother's opinions reflect the values of the Thirties and Forties, plus a reality that exists only in her mind.

But my mind is trapped as well, because I'm morbidly fascinated with my mother's girdle. I blame it and hate it. I hate that it forced my mother to always sit in chairs—never on the floor. It made her name be "Mother," instead of "Mom." It kept my grade school hair in tight braids, my high school body in clothes that were too fussy. It showed me parents who never cuddled, never spooned, never joked with each other. It gave me a false idea of social superiority. Worst of all, it fed me the image of Woman as nonathletic and untouchable.

Our girdles are only as strong as we let them be, I think. But now, here is Barbie with her tiny waist reminding us that what is natural needs to be altered. I find myself buying heels I probably won't wear, searching for a more perfect lipstick color, trying to define a "look" for myself. Breaking out of mental girdles takes years.

How I wish I could have seen my mother's softer side as I was growing up. Now that she's this old, I get occasional glimpses when she's sad or hurting. "Put away that girdle," I want to tell her. "Grandma had it right." It occurs to me that my mother and I are engaged in the same desperate struggle. Both of us are striving to grow up different from our mothers.

The similarity stops there. Mother never questioned the costuming game. Grandma, on the other hand, once she was married, switched to an ungirdled life. She left her things lying about for anyone to see. She wore her stockings rolled down and she doled out love as freely as sugar cookies.

I vow to be more like my soft grandma, no longer swayed by my mother and Barbie and advertisements for abs of steel. It's not easy, but I want to be like my grandma. I want to live the rest of my years casting the shadow of my own shape.

*Grandma Myers holds the author on an
Adirondack porch next to the family dog*

Blue Door Grandma

Hodgepodge, Short Stories and Poetry 10.34 (Fall 2003). Awards: 1st Prize, 10th Anniversary Writing Contest, Stepping Stones (Jul. 31, 2003).

Inspired by Marianna, who knew how to dress unhindered.

en looked out the car window at Grandma's new neighborhood. "How come these houses are glued together?" he asked.

"These are town houses," Dad said. "Your grandma's old house was a country house." He opened the trunk and pulled out Ben's scooter.

"I liked her old house better," Ben said. "It could stand up by itself."

Grandma stood on her new front porch. She was wearing her *Save the Whales* tee-shirt and the swingy skirt with bells on the hem. Her long earrings flashed in the sun. Her eyes flashed even more!

"Uh-oh," said Dad.

"I don't like it here," Grandma said.

"I don't either," said Ben.

Grandma gave them quick hugs and waved them inside. "I told the movers to take these boxes back," she said. "They wouldn't listen to me."

As she walked a path between the boxes to the window, the bells on her skirt jingle-jangled. She tapped on the pane. "Why bother having windows if there aren't any trees and mountains to look at?"

"I see a tree," said Ben.

Grandma turned away from the window with another jangle. "One dinky tree."

Dad thumped a box that said BEDROOM. "We can make the bed and put your rainbow quilt on top. Then you'll like it here."

Grandma shook her head and rubbed her eyes with a tissue. "Go look at that kitchen. Too small."

Ben peeked into the kitchen. "You'll have to make little things," he said. "Like cookies."

She led them out the front door and waved her arms at the houses that were stuck together. "Every house looks the same," she said. "And not one of them looks like me!"

"Could you dress like the doors?" Ben asked. "Red, yellow, green, blue?"

"Your door is a nice blue," Dad said.

"The worst thing is," Grandma said as the bells on her skirt sang a sad song, "no one here knows me. I feel lost."

"Once I was lost," Ben said. "I didn't like it."

Dad took Grandma's hand and squeezed it. "While Ben rides his scooter, we'll hang your Mexican rug by the stairway. We'll put your roaring tiger shower curtain in the bathroom."

"No," Grandma said, "I'm not staying."

The wheels of Ben's scooter whispered on the flat, smooth sidewalk. "I found one good thing," he called. "Scooters go fast here."

"Don't cross the street," Dad called. "Stay where you can see Grandma's front door."

Ben jumped onto his scooter. Down the hill he flew. All at once, he was going too fast!

He was out of control!

He was afraid to jump off!

He was afraid to stay on!

"Help!" Ben yelled. Then, he fell.

Ouch! His knees burned. His elbows stung. Grandma's right, he thought. This is a terrible place.

He wiped away his tears and started up the hill. He saw yellow doors, green doors, red doors, and blue. Which blue door was Grandma's?

He pushed his scooter up the sidewalk that led to the first blue door. "Grandma?" he called.

A woman stepped out. "Be very still," she said. "My sweet finches are here." She raised her binoculars and looked through them. The birds darted across the yard like yellow arrows.

"But I'm lost!" Ben cried. "I'm looking for my grandma. She has a blue door."

The woman put down her binoculars. "We'll find her," she said. "I'll take her my extra bird feeder."

"She won't need a bird feeder," Ben said. "She's not staying."

At the next blue door, a roly-poly man stepped out on the porch. He was playing a silver flute. When the song ended, Ben and the woman clapped their hands. The man waved his flute and bowed.

"Grandma plays that song on her guitar," Ben said.

"She plays Vivaldi?" the man asked. "Her guitar and my flute will play fantastic duets."

"I don't think so," Ben said. "She's not staying."

The bird woman, the flute man, and Ben walked up the street. At the next blue door, a lady came out wearing a long pale, green silk dress. A green jewel glittered at the side of her nose.

Ben sniffed a wonderful smell.

"You smell cumin," the lady said with a smile. "A most lovely spice, cumin."

"We're looking for my grandma," Ben whispered. "She has a blue door."

"I will help," the lady said, "and I'll take to her a jar of cumin."

"She likes to cook," Ben said. "But she's not staying."

Followed by the bird woman, the flute man, and the spice lady, Ben pushed his scooter up the hill. Far away, he saw a person whose skirt swirled around her legs. Her earrings flashed in the sun. She ran down the hill toward him. When they reached each other, she folded him into her arms.

"I was lost," Ben said.

"Ah," Grandma said. "That's terrible."

"Ahem," said a voice.

Ben and Grandma looked up. There were the blue-door people.

The bird woman held out her feeder. "This will bring goldfinches to your new home."

"Thank you," Grandma said, "but I'm not going to stay."

"I'm delighted to find someone who plays Vivaldi," the flute man said, waving his silver flute in the air.

"But I'm not…" Grandma said.

The lady in green silk held out the little jar. "Cumin," she said. "Because you like to cook."

"But…" Grandma said. She sniffed at the jar. Then she smiled.

"My little tree is just big enough to hold this feeder," she told the bird woman.

"Shall we make music on Mondays?" she asked the flute man.

"Let's have tea on Tuesday," she told the spice lady.

The blue-door people waved goodbye and went down the hill.

"Thank you, Ben," Grandma said. "It's nicer here than I expected."

As they walked up the hill together, the sidewalk whispered under the wheels of Ben's scooter. The bells on Grandma's skirt sang a happy song.

The author plays her beloved guitar

A Century of Stitches

Published as "Tiny Stitches Bind the Generations." *Christian Science Monitor* 10 Jun. 1999: 18.

"Help me look for it," my mother said. "Look for what?" I asked. "It's in the sewing cabinet," she said. So not even knowing what we were searching for, I helped her stack everything on her bed: slippery remnants of fabric and patterns left from fifty years of projects, metal zippers in crinkly cellophane, hanks of seed beads purchased at Macy's, wooden spools wound with bright thread, velvet ribbons, and fabric bags with every size of knitting needle and crochet hook.

"Here it is," she said finally. She opened a little box with a sigh of relief. "Here is your grandmother's gold thimble. I want you to have it."

That same day she also gave me a framed piece of embroidery she'd stitched. In it, two ebony-haired Chinese ladies in pink petit point stand on a balcony of pulled-thread work. She named the stitches for me: open trellis, chequer, festoon, wave...

It is beautiful—as fine as any museum piece. Yet I know she learned her stitches when she was a little girl, just as I learned mine, along with pricked fingers and needles that came unthreaded. My daughter went through the same thing. But first stitches turn into mature stitches, even into beautiful stitches. My daughter sews for her own little girl.

Now that I have Grandma's thimble, our combined history of first stitches gains another thirty years. My grandmother took her first stitches when she was five or six. In the 1880s.

Later that day when I was back home, I looked through tattered stitchery books Mother has given me over the years. I saw photos of lacy doilies, crocheted, knitted, or tatted, and blouses with collars and cuffs heavy with black work trimmed with gold thread. Tiny diamond eyelets and flowers shone among satin stitches that adorned petticoats and chemises. Hem-stitched table cloths and runners were done with white thread on white fabric, done as if the embroiderer hardly cared if her stitches were noticed at all.

Women continue to create beauty with needle and thread, even defacing perfectly good fabric, removing threads to make spaces to fill with new threads in feathery designs. In the Sixties, they stitched fancywork onto ordinary denim shirts. In the Seventies, they knotted macrame to cradle the spider plants that swung from every ceiling. In the Eighties, women quilted masterpieces of modern fabrics and modern themes. Today, the fanciest little girls' dresses are still smocked. Tiny seed beads sparkle in jewelry and on fabric and even swing in fringes from the bottoms of lampshades, just as they did in the Twenties.

My grandmother's thimble gleams on my finger and I examine it under the magnifying glass. I see how the gold is marred with dark gouges, which suddenly to my ears resound with the tiny ping of thimble tapping needle thousands, perhaps millions, of times. Tap and push. Tap and push. With this thimble on her finger, my grandmother's needle turned scraps into warm quilts; she replaced the collars and cuffs on my grandfather's shirts; she made gingham dresses for my mother to wear to school. And when she was done with those, she fancied up her pillowcases with lace she'd made herself.

Why did she take the time to fancy something up? Why did she (and why do I) persist in a craft that makes us sit so still, with our eyes downcast? Perhaps we do it, because with downcast eyes, we create works as artistic as any museum piece, as useful as any plowed field, and as precise as an engineer's drawing.

A bond of stitches holds my mother to me and her mother to my daughter who now sews for her own daughter. I find the photograph taken last October in which her baby, my granddaughter, is wearing the christening dress that was made by my grandmother for her first-born child, my mother, in 1906. And no doubt, while Grandma stitched the tiny tucks that decorate the hem she wore the thimble that now warms my finger.

My granddaughter's photo reminds me of other albums and I pull them down from the closet shelf. There is my daughter wearing the latest beaded amulet purse. There I am, modeling the Norwegian cardigan I knitted in blues and grays. And there's the fuchsia hair-

25

pin-lace shawl I made in the Fifties. I see my babies in knitted sweaters and bootees. Here, in an older album, is me again, five years old, in the chiffon dress and shirred bonnet Mother made for me when I was the flower girl in my uncle's wedding. Turning the pages backwards, I find my mother in her 1930 college graduation dress, Bokhara couching on the sleeves. And there is my grandmother in her wedding gown of 1901, cascades of lace on the bodice and the sparkle of beads around the neck.

Every stitch, no matter how simple or how complex, is made with tiny movements of the needle, inserted first in one direction, and then in another. As I close the albums, I savor the wealth of stitches available to me. I think about how the stitches fit into my life.

I live as I stitch. Farfetched thought. But true.

I live one moment at a time. One breath at a time. Stitchery slows me down.

It reminds me that the whole cloth of life is made of tiny moments. First one, then the next, then the next.

This gold thimble has seen one hundred years of stitches. It has seen a century that was shaped by tiny movements and tiny moments. Painstaking stitches, made one…by one…by one.

Harry Myers (author's grandfather),
Mabel Myers (author's grandmother),
and Laura Myers (author's mother)
in the christening dress

Anne Warren Smith

*Four Generations: Laura Forshee (great grandmother),
the author, Mabel Myers (grandmother),*

*Four Generations: The author, mother (Laura Warren),
daughter (Rebecca Smith), and
granddaughter (Sierra Dymond-Smith)*

Getting to the Heart

Persimmon Tree, An Online Magazine of the Arts by Women Over Sixty Issue 31 (Fall 2014). Web.

One day, in the hubbub of the Oaxaca City bus station, we pointed at sentences in our book of important phrases and, with great difficulty, bought round-trip tickets to San Martín Tilcajete. The Oaxaca guidebook had told us we would love this town—known for its whimsical, carved animals.

Once on the bus we relaxed until we realized we had no idea when to get off. Each time the bus stopped we stood up. "San Martín?" we asked in nervous voices. Over and over, the locals gestured us back into our seats. Half an hour later, they whooshed us out the door, leaving us to stand by the side of the road. The person who had gotten off with us pointed west.

We walked the dirt road into town where pastel houses lined the main street. We stepped in and out of little shops, each one a room at the front of someone's home. We were looking for the perfect *alebrije*—the wooden creature we would take back to Oregon. We said *buenos dias* to shopkeepers, then browsed among the animals, large and small, each one ornately painted. We were soon overwhelmed. Should we buy the wonderful, strange giraffe we had seen a few shops back? Surely an iguana was more Mexican.

We agreed we'd seen too many. While we liked some very much, we loved none. Across the street, a building caught our attention with its door of glowing beautiful colors.

"I vote for the giraffe," Jerry said.

The author and her life companion (Jerry)

But I crossed the street and he, being a good sport, followed. As soon as we walked through that colorful door we forgot our tired feet. This gallery was cool, a bit dark after the bright street, but as our eyes adjusted we saw art. Long-finned fish swam among psychedelic turtles and feisty chameleons. Animals posed wearing the horns of another species, or they pranced on fins, or they reached new heights on improbable tails. Jerry stroked the shoulders of an armadillo holding a saxophone. I drifted toward a horse-gazelle, electric blue, that appeared to be leaping into space.

Buenas tardes, a soft voice said, breaking into the cathedral-like silence. A little girl smiled up at me and held out a business card. I looked beyond her into the shadows of the tree-filled courtyard where a young man stood. He waved and said something in Spanish before resuming his carving. The child ran back to her mother who also waved and then turned to rock her baby in a cradle swing. The baby's sweet dusky face drew me from the gallery to the courtyard. I cooed and spoke soft words—in English, of course. The mother smiled and nodded. Baby talk is a universal language.

Jerry, who works with wood at home, drew closer to the carver. He studied the handmade tools with admiration. "What kind of wood?" he asked. "What tree?"

"His mind," Jerry whispered to me, "is so interesting. I wish I could ask if he just picked this up. Did he study with someone? Did it take years? Does he sell in other galleries?"

The gazelle called out to both of us. We carried it to the table in the courtyard and hugged it to show how much we loved it. We paid and shook hands. *Gracias* we said, but the word vibrated with sadness. We had found our *alebrije,* but we had lost a chance to get to know its creators.

Those final minutes in San Martín had tugged me back into childhood. Jerry's face reflected mine— we both understood the frustration of being voiceless.

We had grown up in families that did not let us speak.

The first thing my new friend did that was different—she rang her own doorbell. We waited, hugging heavy book bags and shivering in the January chill. It was 1955, and after lonely months in this new high school I finally had a friend.

"A minute," someone called from the other side of the door.

"It's just me," Joan called back.

"Oh, just you," The door swung inward. The woman facing us had been trying to pin a maid's cap onto her flyaway orange hair. Her blouse needed tucking. She glowered.

"This is Miss Murray," Joan said as we hastened into the warmth.

"And this is the famous Anne." Miss Murray gave up on the hat and placed her hands on her hips. "Now, when you see her room, remember it's never looked so nice. She finally cleaned it."

"Don't tell on me, Miss Murray," Joan said.

Joan could say "don't" to an adult. My stomach lurched.

"Ah, and you're a quiet one," Miss Murray said.

"A relief from me," Joan said. "I never stop talking." She led the way toward a room that held square furniture in chrome and plastic, wall-to-wall carpeting, and modern canvases on white walls. The view beyond the living room windows caught me—a lake! A complete, sweet, ice-covered lake!

Joan put her hand on my arm before I could speak. "Where is she?" she whispered to Miss Murray.

Miss Murray put her fingers to her lips and pointed at a closed door.

Joan turned abruptly. She pulled me away from the living room and up carpeted stairs, narrow and winding. Framed watercolors of tilted buildings and sharp flowers filled the staircase walls. "My mother painted all these," she said as we climbed.

I stopped to look at a picture of a face—all angles and three slanted eyes.

At the top of the stairs, Joan opened the door to her room and shrugged out of her coat. She dropped her book bag and her coat onto the plush blue carpet. "Look here." She opened the closet door and exposed a mountain of clothes, shoes, papers, and books. "I really did clean up my room. Here it all is."

I had to grin.

Joan and I curled up on the twin beds with our school books and resumed our conversation about her current heartthrob. Chatting with a friend—how sweet. Happiness poured into me. At this new school close to New York City, where the kids seemed so articulate—

so opinionated about everything—I hardly opened my mouth. Of course, at home, nothing had changed. There, my silence was expected.

A few minutes later, a crackle and a tinny voice came out of a box next to the door. Joan ran to it and pushed a button.

"Ask Anne, does she like artichokes."

Fruits and vegetables tumbled through my head until I settled on one. Mother, making a special salad, had showed us something that looked like a dark green egg. We had nibbled at chunks of buttery soft flesh as she cut it away from the brown pit.

"Oh, yes," I said.

"She adores artichokes," Joan told the intercom.

Adores. A Hollywood word. I drew in my breath.

"What does she like with it?" the metallic voice asked.

My heart stopped beating. Long silence.

"Mayo, mustard, lemon juice, or butter," Joan prompted.

None of these suited the artichoke in my mind. "Mayonnaise?" I ventured.

Later, at Joan's dinner table, classical music wafted out of hidden speakers. Ice sparkled in water glasses. Lighted candles stood in silver holders.

The mother, the artist!, patted the chair beside

her and asked me to sit down. Dark-haired and pretty, she wore a scarlet silk blouse and a heavy string of pearls with her long black skirt. Only three buttons held her blouse together. She was my first mother with cleavage.

"So this is the Anne I've been hearing about," she said in a Bette Davis voice.

Joan's father made a little bow. "Velcome to our house," he said. Joan had told me that he had designed this house. Pictures of it had been in *Architectural Digest*.

Joan's brother scowled and muttered, "Hi." He was the studious one. He planned to be a doctor.

Joan grabbed her napkin and tossed it across her lap. I did the same as Miss Murray brought in a basket of warm bread and went around the table offering it like a waitress. When she got to me, she winked.

A small plate to the north of my forks held a thing that reminded me of a little Christmas tree. Everyone had one; this tree was mine. Surely this wasn't something to eat! I quickly decided I had not seen it. Later I would say I was too full.

As Miss Murray brought in lamb and roasted potatoes, I struggled through shyness to answer their questions. "My dad works for International Paper in the city." "Yes, he takes the seven-forty train." "We moved here from Ticonderoga. I was born there. I lived there sixteen years." I sipped my water and set the glass down on the white cloth with shaking fingers.

"She's way ahead in French class," Joan said. "My French is so bad," she continued, "I had to go to French camp last summer. I had to miss tennis camp."

Did summer camp come in more flavors than Girl Scout? That was news to me, but the green thing on the little plate kept drawing my attention. Steam rose from its pointed top. The others were doing things to theirs. They had tipped them on their sides and scattered or stacked their leaves beside them.

Somehow, they could eat and talk, too. They discussed a collection of Italian art at the museum. They talked about someone called Leonard Bernstein who taught music at Tanglewood. Joan's brother mentioned the rabbi and temple.

My bite of lamb lost its flavor. Joan's family was Jewish! My mother was going to tighten her lips and sigh. She and Dad would talk in low voices. They would try to take away my only friend!

They were all looking at me. "College applications," someone repeated. "Where will you apply?"

I set down my fork. I drew a long breath. "I want to go to Middlebury to study languages."

"But even if they accept her, she can't go there," Joan said. "She has to go to Cornell."

"Cornell is a fine university." Her father cut a piece of lamb and took a bite.

"Has to go there?" As her mother leaned toward me I forced my eyes away from her low-cut blouse.

I looked down at my hands, now twisting in my lap. "My brother's at Cornell. My parents went there. My mother says I will go there to take Home Economics."

Joan thumped her fist on the table. "So she can be the perfect wife!" Her voice grew louder. "She should be studying languages. She should follow her passion."

My lungs filled with excitement. Passion! Another star-studded word.

They got me to tell them about the recent field trip to the United Nations. How through the headphones I had heard the translators instantly turn a speech into Chinese, German, French, and more. "They have to be so good," I said.

Joan's mother nodded. "The future of the world could depend on how well they translate. Nations talking to each other could lead us to world peace."

They said I had high standards. Vision. They said Joan was fortunate to have a friend like me! They thought I was something!

At that moment Joan nudged my arm. "You forgot your artichoke."

The music from the stereo was the only sound in the room. Everyone looked at my plate.

"Just see the way Joan puts her leaves," her mother finally said. "Her dresser drawers look like that plate."

"And your plate shows that you're an artist." Joan said. It was true. The leaves on her mother's plate swirled in graceful patterns. Joan pulled my plate closer and showed me how to get started. "This part is slow," she said. "But it's all worth it when you get to the heart."

"We're delighted to introduce you to something new." Joan's mother offered bread to everyone and the conversation rushed on to other matters.

Joan and I took turns finishing my artichoke. She was right about the heart.

Home from school the next day, I walked through my family's unlocked front door into a room filled with antique china cabinets and chairs upholstered in velvet. Beveled mirrors hung in heavy wooden frames next to white silk lamp shades. Mother's collection of Dresden figurines and Italian glass paperweights filled every table. *Ladies Home Journal* and *Woman's Day* were heaped on the stool beside Mother's chair.

At dinner, Dad talked about office politics. Mother described a shopping trip to find drapery fabric. My voice had no place at this table. Did all the other dinner tables in Westchester County bubble with ideas and opinions and discussions? Did all the other kids get to talk?

When my parents asked about my visit to Joan, I swallowed any words about Leonard Bernstein or rabbis. I didn't mention the lake or the maid. But I had to let them know that I had feasted at a different kind of table.

I drew a long breath and dove in. "I learned how to eat an artichoke."

Mother clicked her tongue in dismay. "I should have served them before now."

"We talked about all kinds of things," I continued. "They thought it was great that I like French so much." I looked away from my parents and down at my fork. "I told them I want to be a UN interpreter. They liked the idea."

Mother's polished nails tapped the table top. "They were just being polite."

I tried one more time. "They think it's good to do what you love..."

"You'll take home economics," she said. "It worked for me."

Back home in Oregon, Jerry and I are eating artichokes. I settle mine onto the black plate and dollop mayonnaise beside it.

Our beautiful *alebrije* balances on a nearby table, its gazelle-like body brilliant blue against the white bricks behind it. I raise a leaf in toast to the Mexican woodcarver and to his young wife. Will we ever go back to see them? And if we do, will we carry more words?

Perhaps we will. We have moved beyond *sí* and *dónde està el baño*?, and we are both in love with Irma, our pretty Spanish teacher. Last night in front of twenty classmates, after I stumbled through, "I live in Corvallis. I am a teacher for writers," Irma clapped her hands and sang out, "*¡Magnífico! ¡Estupendo!*"

Irma works hard to hear the meaning behind our halting speech. I've decided that she and I have that in common as teachers. We are both translators—helping to turn a stumbling phrase into meaningful communication. She is the latest of those who over the years have helped me break through silence to speak out, to reach out, to others. But, of course, Joan and her family did it first.

Jerry's voice pulls me back to the present. "I have this idea for building a cabinet."

I should ask where on earth we will put this cabinet, but instead, I watch his pencil move across scratch paper. He says the slender walnut cabinet will hold wine glasses. The doors will be quilted maple, coopered, and unusual. He wants it to have long, graceful legs. I understand that it will be beautiful. Of course, we'll find a place for it.

As we progress with our artichokes, the discarded leaves reveal our personalities: Jerry's are helter-skelter; mine form tight lines with each leaf nestled into the one before it. We touch each meaty leaf to the mayo, scrape off the good stuff with our teeth, and return the tooth-marked leaf to the plate. We practice Spanish sentences for next week's class, correcting ourselves in mid-word, taking forever to say the simplest things.

"I am writing a story," I say in Spanish. *"Escribo de mi madre."*

"About what?" Jerry asks.

"About my mother."

He knows exactly how important my story will be. *"¡Magnífico!"* he exclaims.

"¡Estupendo!" I grin at him and the dog who thinks our giddiness is about her rushes to us for patting.

Eating an artichoke creates spaces in our conversation. We tip over the words as we tip over the leaves, —looking for what is inside. Savory moments later, when we get there, we gently scrape away the choke. This part is slow, my friend Joan said years ago. But it's all worth it when you get to the heart.

One Night at
Camp Kilowan

Camp Fire Leadership Magazine 53: 4 (Summer 1974). Camp Fire Girls, Inc.

Being a Camp Fire leader isn't always what it's cracked up to be. Physical anguish and mental cruelty are harsh terms, but they come to mind when I think of the time my twelve fourth graders and I went to Camp Kilowan for our first overnight.

At the beginning, I was all for the idea—in fact it was my idea. My group had recently been formed from two smaller ones and consisted, for the most part, of extremely active, needing-to-be-noisy girls. While my optimistic self mused that the pure fun of an overnight away from home could provide the cement for happy companionship for the rest of the year, the pessimistic side of me reserved the warmest cabin available (one with a fireplace and windows that actually close). I firmly stated that we would stay for just one night, and, knowing that merely boiling water might be a big accomplishment, our meals were planned to be simple.

Our council had scheduled our group camping weekend for November 2 and 3, which to a non-

Oregonian may sound like the dead of winter. It isn't, however. Usually our misty rains have begun, but temperatures are in the 40s and 50s and with the raingear that every schoolgirl in the valley has in her closet by the time she is in the fourth grade, we expected to be quite comfortable. Unfortunately, the day before our camp-out the heavens cleared and temperatures dropped to the 20s.

"Of course we're still going—isn't it nice to see the sun," I repeated into the phone. "Just bring extra blankets, mittens and scarves." With those adjustments and with extra packages of hot chocolate, we were ready.

I know now that before we'd even climbed into the cars, I gained in my understanding of nine year olds. For one thing, I had believed that my own child was the only one still requiring a "Blankee." "Oh, Mrs. Smith, I'll never get a wink of sleep without Teddy," said my toughest, loudest, most competitive girl, and off she flew on a borrowed bike.

Sooner than expected, we got it all together. The lists were covered with check marks, and gear, girls and Teddy were stowed away. Off we went, leaving my normally staid neighborhood sounding like an empty tomb in comparison to the din we had closed into the cars.

Forty-five minutes later, as we drove between the totem poles into Camp Kilowan, late afternoon sunlight glistened on the lush ferns and evergreens. The girls who had been there before sang out the landmarks:

"There's the swimming pond. And Kobie's Tree." (Kobie is a "squirrel" who writes messages to campers.) "Teal Lodge," they sang out, "and Pill Palace." A turn in the narrow road brought us within sight of Bonnie Briar, half hidden beneath tall Douglas Firs. A trim, square building, it contained just enough floor space for our fourteen cots and one enormous table.

Stowing gear and unrolling sleeping bags was our first chore. Unhappily, this created an element of discord that lasted for several hours. Of the twelve girls, three of them didn't care who they slept by, that is, as long as Jenette could be by Bev and vice versa, and Christine by an adult. No-one wanted the place by the door (a slug was crawling up it) or the windows (they looked a little spidery). Five girls wanted their cots by Kathleen (impossible of course) but each one also wanted someone special on her other side which made it hopeless. For a while, our snug abode looked like the setting for a crazy sort of cotillion, as beds were lifted, turned, tipped and moved from here to there. Even worse were the sounds, which reminded me of the day the nursery school ran out of graham crackers.

Soon however, the plunging temperature diverted their interest from social concerns to physical and the girls who were new to camping reacted by huddling despondently into their jackets. I began to coax them to get busy and active. The cooks set up for hamburgers and the fire-builders started a fire crackling in the fire ring beside the cabin. All would have been swell if the sun hadn't just then clunked out behind the nearby

Anne Warren Smith

mountain. Suddenly branches and boulders appeared under our feet causing us to stumble and bang shins. No -one could tell if her meat was cooked and it was too cold to enjoy carrot sticks, apples or milk. Our feet were like lumps of ice and so were our seats if we sat down. If we hadn't been too cold to stand still, this would have been the ideal time to deliver my famous sermon entitled "Cheerfulness in the Face of Adversity." (The girls call it "If you can't say something pleasant don't say anything at all.")

Somehow, the ordeal ended. Dishes were washed and we used some hot water for liquid Jell-O which made us all feel better. Then off we marched to the Rec Hall to sing and roast marshmallows with other groups. By getting as close as possible to the roaring fire, some feeling began to return to our feet and by the time we walked back to Bonnie Briar spirits were high and the cabin resounded with uproarious songs and jokes. Once in bed, the girls gazed delightedly at the beautiful fire in the fireplace, sang every song again, and tried to make up a ghost story that everyone hadn't already heard.

My helper and I, delightfully unaware of what lay ahead, propped our feet on the hearth, leaned back in rickety chairs and sipped hot tea. For the moment, we had no decisions to make; specifically, no need to create new ways to get warm.

"However will we get the girls quiet enough to go to sleep?" Molly asked. I suspected that she had a headache, but I looked at my watch anyway. It was time for calming down, so we sang quieter songs. Then, after reminders about early morning etiquette, some compliments about improved dispositions and an important hugging and tucking ceremony for each, they were almost all asleep.

A few minutes later, after banking the fire, we snuggled into our sleeping bags too. Molly was asleep almost immediately and I reflected jealously on her ability to relax. My mind continued to spin as I thought over the day's experiences. Then I went mentally through the next day's plans. Finally, I lay there conjecturing how long the fire might last, which reminded me of two phone calls I had received that morning from mothers: one concerned that we might go to sleep with a fire going, the other worried that I might let the fire go out. I planned to do both having been reassured by my husband that our cabin was far from air-tight and we weren't likely to asphyxiate. Also, I knew that once I was warm in bed it would take more than a dead fire to get me out again.

However, as I lay there, I began to hear weird noises. Mutterings were coming from Cindy's vicinity, so I raised up on one elbow to peer at her. From the other end of the room came snuffly snores, probably Trisha. Beside me Christine began to clutch wildly at her bag and I reached over to help. Then I snuggled back in again, recoiling from the shock of my icy arm.

So it went. For fifteen minutes, I would doze, then something would make me poke my head out. A log rolled in the fireplace so I watched it a while to make sure it was all right. Then someone began to moan. At least three different times I stuck my head out, waiting for the next moan so I could find the girl who was so terribly uncomfortable. When at last I had her located, I struggled out of my bag and on highest possible tiptoes to keep my feet from freezing fast to the floor, I bent over Karen with my flashlight.

"What's the matter?" I asked. A sleepy "Hm-m-m" told me I had the wrong girl. "What's the matter?" I said again, this time to the room in general. No answer. "Go to sleep," I said, just in case anyone but me was awake, and made a dive for my bag.

My goose bumps were barely smoothed out when the moans began again. Furiously, I looked out. This time there could be no mistake. Four beds away, I saw a mysteriously glowing undulating mound. As the glow moved upward, I recognized with relief the double ring of a flashlight. The moans were coming unmistakably from my daughter who had chosen this time to search for something inside her bag.

"Amy!" I called. Of course she couldn't hear me, so out I struggled again, putting on the patient smile which comes more easily for other people's children.

Amy was relieved to see my smile. "There's a bump in my bag and I'm terribly cold," she said. With chattering teeth, I straightened the bag, arranged her jacket over her feet, gave her a pat, and with the agility that comes from practice, leaped once again into my sleeping bag. Consumed with curiosity, I held my watch up to the remaining firelight. Unbelievable. I'd been up all night but it was barely 11:30. There was still a chance for a good night's sleep—I resolved to imitate Molly's relaxed and apparently deaf slumber. For three blissful hours I succeeded and then awoke with sinking heart. Someone was sobbing.

"Appendicitis," I thought. "We'll never make it to a hospital in time."

"Mrs. Smith, Kathleen is crying," said a very worried voice. The other girls knew as I did that Kathleen does not cry easily.

"Kathleen, what is the matter?"

"I'm so cold," she groaned. "Oh, I'm so cold."

Relief and determination buoyed me up out of my bag. "All right," I announced. "First, I will put on my shoes and jacket (I was getting smart) and then I will fix everything."

A few minutes later, the fire was blazing and crackling. There were extra blankets on the cold places, bags straightened, flashlights located, Kleenexes offered and extra socks on cold feet. Then, for good measure, I topped off the activity with a short song and dance routine in striped pajamas in front of the fire. "Oh, Mrs. Smith, what a nut you are," was the comment I heard before they pulled their heads like turtles into their bags and went to sleep.

It was 8:00 before we woke again. Compared to the experiences of our previous day, cooking breakfast and getting ready for our hike were easy. At noon, when we stopped to sit on the big logs that form the rings of the Grand Council Fire, we ate our lunches in quiet peacefulness. It's true, we were tired, but I think that also we were finally in harmony with each other and with our surroundings. Suddenly our peace was shattered by a shriek of delight. "It's snowing, it's snowing!" Around the fire ring they cavorted, waving sandwiches in the air, laughing as the flakes settled in their hair.

"Wait 'til we tell everyone we had lunch in a snowstorm," Sheila said gleefully, and even though in ten minutes the flakes had turned to familiar rain, the snow is what we remember.

Kilowan Collage used by permission
By Carri Heisler on "Kilowan Memories Blog"
at https://kilowan.wordpress.com

Reeds Shall Bend

Memoir Journal 1.2 (Summer 2008).

S chroon Lake chilled my hot feet, washed and shrank them, as it chatted with the dock pilings below me. The Adirondacks gave up their green and then turned dark and blended with the sky. I became once again my father's child, dipping feet into water at the end of a dock. In the eighty years my father had known it the contours of this lake had not changed. In these waters, he had learned to swim. In these mountains, he'd learned to dream.

As more stars winked on, I thought about the last time I was at here at Schroon. That night—two years ago—Dad and I fitted the oars into the rowboat and took it out in the last light.

We told the others we planned to watch the moon rise. I, however, always had ulterior motives for spending time alone with my father. He was a puzzle; I'd never gotten close to him. He believed the concerns of parents were private, so he didn't discuss things with us children. Besides that, over the years he'd become so deaf our conversations consisted of him talking, me nodding and smiling. Or even worse, he misunderstood things. "But you told me this," he'd insist, and then I'd try to make clear (for a man who couldn't hear) what was true and what was not. We learned to avoid feelings, or subtleties, or musings. We stayed with the facts.

"You see that fish jump?" he asked as he rowed away from shore that night. His oars paused and dribbled strings of silver pearls into the water.

I shook my head. I could seldom see what he could see—the deer standing on the other bank, the hawk circling above the trees, a fish flashing through deep water.

"Follow my finger with your eye," he said. "See those ripples?" I nodded, not sure, but thinking, yes, maybe I had the right ripples. "Now, watch," he said. "It might jump again."

We waited. After a while, he dipped the oars, rowed on. I was used to nothing happening, but I also knew you had to do it that way. Wait, and watch, and listen. You might see something wonderful.

Conversations with my dad were one-sided but not boring. He knew his chemicals—he was a chemical engineer—but also he knew geology, politics, history, and geography. He could name every tree, every constellation, every bird. Even in his eighties, he could instantly convert meters to inches, rods to acres. He never forgot the volume of a keg or how many sheets in a ream.

Several weeks after our evening boat ride, he

was diagnosed with inoperable cancer. I flew every couple of months from Oregon to New York State to where he and Mother lived in Westchester County, downstate and a world apart from Schroon Lake and the Adirondack Mountains.

One day in June, the two of us went to the library. He thumbed through *The Wall Street Journal*. In a few minutes, he would calculate his gains and losses and adjust his net worth, all in his head. He always finished with a little shrug or a little smile. He'd watched the market go up and down so many years, nothing flustered him.

He shrugged that day, closed the newspaper, folded it, returned it to the rack. He stood a moment gazing at nothing, his chest caved in, his elbows jutting out from scrawny arms. He'd lost forty pounds, but that very morning he told me, "They were wrong about this being cancer. They said six months, but I'm still here." My mouth had dropped open. He'd walked away before I could think of how to answer.

I touched his arm. If he looked at me, watched my lips, he could "hear" me. "Shall we go home?"

"Not yet." His voice was too loud in the library. "How do you find a poem?"

I was mystified. A poem? My dad? "Who wrote it? Someone famous?"

"American poet," he answered. "Yes, I think so. Famous."

"Come with me," I said.

He hadn't understood. I beckoned. He followed. In the literature section I moved to poetry, hoping to be quick because he was panting now, in pain. My eyes raced across the shelves to find anthologies. American Poets. I pulled out a book.

"Bryant," he said. "William Cullen." I found his name in the index and turned to the poem. "To a Water-fowl." He nodded and bent close to read it. It took me a few minutes to realize I'd happened upon the very poem he wanted.

I read over his shoulder. "Whither midst falling dew...dost thou pursue thy solitary way?" My dad loved the solitary way. He'd always wanted to leave crowded Westchester County and go back to the Adirondacks.

"All day thy wings have fanned," I read, "at that far height, the cold, thin atmosphere." If he was going to like one poem, this would be it.

We made a copy of the poem and walked to the car where he slumped, exhausted, into the passenger seat. I paused before putting the key into the ignition. Dying was surely at the top of the long list of things we could never talk about. But I had to ask a question before starting the car. He'd never hear me over the noise of the motor.

"We studied this poem in school," he said, looking down at the paper in his hands. "I knew it by heart."

"Would you like someone to read it," I asked,

"… at your memorial service?" I glanced at him, looked past him out the car window, finally glanced back.

He was nodding. "Good," he said.

I turned the key in the ignition as if my pulse were normal, as if my hands weren't trembling. That moment of honest talk marked the beginning of a journey for me, a migration as mysterious as that of the waterfowl that traveled alone in Bryant's poem.

When I was a child, back when he could still hear my voice, we lived upstate in Ticonderoga, at the north end of Lake George, not far from Schroon Lake. I must have been ten the day he and I took a rowboat onto Lake George, our destination the island in the middle. "Want to row?" he asked.

"Me?"

"Yes, you."

"You bet." I scooted to sit beside him. He showed me how to hold the oars and how to brace my heels. He moved to the stern. I was on my own.

At first, the oars twisted out of my hands and banged the side of the boat. I fought to make them move together. I learned to push down to lift the blades and then push forward before dipping them once more. The boat groaned and balked. An oar leaped out of its oarlock. Dad helped me put it back in.

When I got the rhythm right, the noises told me

so. *Creak*, went the oarlocks as I pushed my hands down and away. *Splash*, went the blades into the water. *Groan*, went the oarlocks as I pulled with all my might, bracing my heels against the floor of the boat. *Creak, splash, groan.* I was doing fine except for one thing. The island, our destination, was now in front of me. I was pulling us back toward shore.

Dad reached for an oar and in a minute had us moving toward the island again. "You can keep looking over your shoulder at the island," he said, "but it's better to choose something to watch in front of you, on shore. A reference point. Pick out a building or a big tree. Something that won't move."

"You choose for me."

"It has to be from your eyes."

"That green boathouse," I told him. "Right behind your ear."

"Good," he said. "Keep it behind my ear. If you can do that, we'll keep going toward the island."

I checked it out. He was right. It was like being able to walk through a maze blindfolded. Or like guessing the future!

"Don't move your ear," I said.

He grinned at me.

I pushed and tugged on the oars. My former rhythm had disappeared and every time I got it back the boathouse slipped away from Dad's ear. "When I get good enough," I told him. "I'll never have to turn around."

"Yes, you will," he said, "just to make sure. So you don't bump into something."

"Like an island?"

"Like an island," he answered.

A few days after we found the poem at the library, I returned to Oregon. I bought a book of poems with "To a Waterfowl" in it and read it more carefully. Some of the lines suited Dad; some did not. "There is a Power whose care teaches thy way," and "He who...guides through the boundless sky thy certain flight..." I figured Bryant was talking about God and, for my dad, that wasn't right.

Mother coaxed Dad to church for Christmas Eve or Easter Sunday. That was enough for him. One time I visited, the minister had come. Dad had gone to bed to rest that painful area in his back so the minister went upstairs and pulled a chair close to his bed. "You probably have things on your mind," I heard him say in a voice that Dad could surely hear. "Anything you'd like to talk about?"

Silence.

Finally, Dad's voice. "How about those Mets," he said. "You watch last night's game?"

I sent the book of poems to Dad. Was he a one-poem man? I didn't know. But possibly he'd look through the book and find a better one. Maybe he was having second thoughts about "Waterfowl." I certainly was.

Maybe, he'd talk to Mother about the poem and why it meant so much to him. But, between them, things were awful. When I visited, I heard all their regrets and anger spew out in arguments about what to eat for lunch or whether to call in hospice or who could do the yard work. Mother blamed him for years of keeping her a housewife. He blamed her for years of keeping them downstate. "My biggest regret," he wrote, "is that I never got back to the mountains. There's nothing to do here…"

A neighbor phoned me. "I'm not sure your father is getting enough to eat." Her voice was apologetic, embarrassed. "He says your mother won't cook for him."

I called Mother. "He doesn't like anything I fix," she said. "He asks for ridiculous things. Then he doesn't eat them."

"He's sick," I said.

"I don't care," she answered. "He's impossible."

A dietician friend suggested easy snacks: hard-boiled eggs, chicken, and cheese, cut into bite-sized chunks. I sent Power Bars and plastic bags of raisins and granola. I knew, however, all this was stupid. He needed more than food.

I wrote him a careful letter and sent it by way of a kind neighbor. I said I knew he and Mother weren't getting along. I told him I wanted something better for him. I offered my house and Oregon wild places, my local hospice, the hospital, my favorite doctor. I offered him a chance to live in a home that was peaceful and loving.

"What would people think," he wrote back, "if I left your mother here alone? Don't worry about me. A long time ago, I decided I could live without love."

Live without love! I studied his handwriting and the way he made his capital letters. Memories crowded in: the times they'd sniped at each other, interrupted and corrected each other, foiled each other's hopes and dreams. It wasn't pretty, but I'd never translated it into a life without love!

If ever you needed love, it would be when you were dying! I scrubbed the shower tiles and later went out to tramp in the forest trying to breathe through the anger and despair that fought in my chest. He HAD to come live with me. But I knew he'd say no. Also, I knew I was offering a poor substitute. Oregon. Not the Adirondacks.

I wrote another letter, leaving out any reference to love or a failed marriage or a life filled with regrets. "I have an idea about your ashes," I wrote. "Half can go into the Columbarium next to Mother. We could take the other half upstate, to a place you choose. It would be easy to do and it would make us feel good. What do you think?"

Once again, I'd crossed into an emotional conversation with my dad. Talking about the ashes. His ashes! His last rites! Back in Oregon, I held my breath. Had I gone too far?

When I got to New York in August, he was determined, in spite of his weakness, to take me crabbing on a friend's boat in the Hudson. He was fascinated with the crab's life cycle. "They have to move upstream and downstream, in and out of saline water at just the right time for molting, and again, for fertilization," he said.

"How do they know where to go?" I asked. "And when?"

"Nature," he said, and then he stopped. "Water temperature." He shrugged. "I don't think anyone really knows for sure."

Migrations intrigued him: crabs, caribou, salmon, and, of course, birds. Back when we lived upstate, he had banded evening grosbeaks and exchanged letters with a man in North Carolina who recorded the same birds. When he visited Oregon, he watched the sanderlings scoot like wind-up toys on our beaches. He sent me an article about them; he wanted me to know that "my" birds most likely flew to Hawaii for the winter.

After we discussed the crabs, Dad got to talking

about the hill above his old home near Schroon Lake. It was called Charlie Hill by the locals, a place where Dad's family owned a wood lot and where he'd often hunted. "There's a large boulder," he said, "where we always stationed a man to watch and listen. The rest of us drove the deer up the hill toward him." He paused. "That's the place," he said finally.

I was silent. Wondering. "The place for...?"

"The ashes."

The minister read Bryant's poem at the memorial service. "All day thy wings have fanned," he said in that clear voice that Dad would have been able to hear. "And soon that toil shall end; soon shalt thou find a summer home." I closed my ears to the lines about God and thought instead about taking the ashes to Schroon. Had that plan helped him get through the final days of a life that held no love?

The arrangements for taking the ashes to the Adirondacks took months. For one thing, we had to wait till winter left the mountains. It was the following August before my brother and I were able to travel at the same time from different parts of the country to meet at Mother's. The three of us drove the Northway past Albany and Glens Falls and checked into the motel on Schroon Lake.

That night as I unpacked, I stroked the velvet

bag that held Dad's ashes. In the soft gray fabric, the ashes were heavy, crumbly, crunchy. "Almost home," I whispered. "And soon that toil shall end...reeds shall bend soon o'er thy sheltered nest." I tucked the bag into my suitcase and walked the path to the lake.

Two years had passed since the night Dad and I rowed out to watch the moon rise. Sitting on the dock, I shivered as the water chilled my feet and the light left the mountains. Far out on the lake, a fish jumped and I waited and watched to see if it would jump again. Waiting and watching were like trying to figure out who my father really was. I wished I'd asked him what he thought about God. If it wasn't God who guided us, what was it?

He would have changed the subject.

The moon rose and cast a golden path across the lake. With the light came the realization that I had some answers, after all. For one, it was okay to let some things be mysteries. I was never going to know my father as well as I wanted to.

But I knew a few things. I knew he would have said he believed in a natural progression, the path that crosses from birth to death. He believed some things need time, whether it is teaching a child to look at a point on shore for guidance, or teaching her to watch and wait for answers that don't come right away. Perhaps he viewed his marriage with that same tolerance, since in nature perfection is rare and over time things decay. He would have said that our lives reflect the rising and setting of suns and moons, the changing of seasons, and the rhythms of the great migrations.

He was, however, wrong about one thing. He'd overlooked part of nature's equation—the part about love.

Love had brought him back to his summer home—the place of his birth. Love for a poem memorized in high school. Love for the miraculous ways of crabs, and animals, and birds. Love for certain lakes and mountains. Love that flowed from me to him and back again, drawing us close together after all.

*The author's father
("Bob" Thurman C. Warren)
and the author*

The author's father ("Bob" Thurman C. Warren)
at a family wedding a few years before his death

How to Tell Them?

Before my parents arrived in Oregon for the 1985 Christmas visit, my ex-husband-to-be and I agonized over what to do—mainly, how to tell them. Every time we pictured it, we knew we couldn't tell them at all! Telling would tear apart everything my family cherished: pretension, appearance, conformity. Maintenance was a big thing: my parents had set some kind of record for maintaining an awful marriage.

In a light moment, we considered inviting them back every year for Christmas week during which we'd pretend nothing had changed. One of us would keep the house; the other would move back in for a while. We knew we couldn't pull it off. But the alternative—telling them—was unthinkable.

In the meantime, we did what maintenance we could do: polished the silver, washed the windows, dusted far back inside the cupboards. He repaired the broken veneer on the dresser, and I wound the antique clock and set it. It was expected that the clock, like everything else, would be in good working condition.

Our daughters came home from college, sworn to secrecy. They rolled their eyes at us, but they also knew my parents.

The arrival date was December 15, my mother's birthday. "We can't tell them on her birthday," I said.

He agreed. "The sixteenth?"

"We're cutting the tree that day. It's such a big deal."

On the seventeenth we would work at the food bank, carrying packages to families. We couldn't ruin that.

On the 18th there was another reason. And so it went.

Not telling them wasn't so hard after they arrived: my mother's light conversation filled every space. Every day had an activity. At the coast we ate chowder and poked our fingers into tide pools. Back home, our daughters and their friends baked cookies and filled the house with laughter and good smells. One evening, we showed slides of my husband's South American work sites. "Gone a lot, aren't you?" my dad asked him. We both almost spoke and then were silent. On Christmas Eve we filed into a church pew and sang carols. We opened presents together the next morning, four of us knowing this was the last time...two of us still without a clue.

It was during the present opening that I realized that, had they known the truth, my parents wouldn't have given my husband a present. Were they going to think we'd planned it so we'd get the presents first? Through it all, my mother talked of the newest kitchen gadgets in someone's new house.

Christmas dinner was traditional chicken and dumplings, sweet potatoes, cherry pie. As Mother and I prepared the salad, she described decorations hung that year in Rockefeller Center, three thousand light years away from Oregon. I scraped carrots in vicious strokes while we wasted kitchen moments—the best moments of all—wasted them in small talk. For the millionth time, I wished for a mother who'd stop talking about how things looked. I needed a mother who'd agree it was okay to want happiness in a marriage. But this mother, if she stopped to look beyond the surface, would see the unmendable tatters of her own marriage. How could I ask her to do that?

Each night, he and I lay next to each other in the bed we'd shared so long—careful now, careful not to touch.

December 28th, he returned to South America. My parents rode with us to the Eugene Airport, where he and I clung to each other at the gate. "I should have helped you tell them," he said.

"I can do it," I said, but I wasn't sure. As he walked through the gate, however, the unwifely part of me rejoiced. Another calendar milestone! In a few more months, once the divorce was final, I wouldn't have this exhausting task any more—seeing him off, saying goodbye.

With my mother and father in the car, I drove north on 99 through Junction City, into the town of Monroe. That year had been hard on Monroe; the newspapers had called it Oregon's Appalachia. My mother talked on, describing Christmas decorations in the mansions at Williamsburg. All at once, I drove onto the shoulder and parked next to a ramshackle cafe, surprising her into silence. "Dad. Mother," I said, talking fast, before she could speak again. "I have something to tell you."

The tree featured in the story

The Gift Oft Scorned

To Inspire: Gifts. Monograph of the Mountain Vista Unitarian Universalist Congregation (Apr. 2014).

N o jokes about cardboard and glue," I want to tell the folks who will receive my gifts. "Don't even mention turning these into doorstops."

My recipe, more than a century old, was handed down from Grandma Myers to Mother, and then to me. The recipe card, like the backs of elderly hands, is spotted brown.

Just as Grandma did, I locate the only container that's large enough—the big roaster pan. Into it I dump candied cherries, pineapples, and fruits and peels. I top the jeweled fruits with seeded and seedless raisins, sticky dates, and luscious figs. For the batter, I blend spices, eggs, flour, brown sugar, butter, and molasses. After spooning the batter over it all, I set my utensils aside. Only bare hands can do the rest, and I remember my small hands working next to Mother's, the two of us bent over the same pan.

I smooth the dark mixture into loaf pans. For the next hours, the oven sends out smells of molasses, cloves, coffee, cinnamon, allspice, and nutmeg.

I wrap the cooled cakes four times—twice with waxed paper, twice with aluminum foil. In late December, I add ribbons and tags.

The loaves go on the hall table, to be placed into the hands of friends.

Fruitcake.

And much, much more.

Back row: Laura "Nonna" Christman (author's great grandmother), Harry Myers (author's grandfather), Mabel Myers (author's grandmother)
Front row: Laura Myers (author's mother), George Myers (author's uncle)

Thank Goodness for Mr. Bear!

Innovation Abstracts 21.20 (Sep. 24, 1999). National Institute for Staff and Organizational Development.

Society of Children's Book Writers and Illustrators Bulletin (Jan./Feb. 1999).

I've taught writing classes a long, long time. I began when I was eight. Back then, it was dolls and stuffed animals who sat in rows facing my blackboard. I taught them homonyms. "Pair, pare," I told them and wrote the two words on the board. "And sometimes they come in threes! Look at this, Class! Rain, rein, reign." I wrote all over the chalkboard—hundreds of homonyms grouped around a message to my brother, "ERASE THIS AND I'LL TELL ABOUT YOU KNOW WHAT!!!"

Margaret Rose, my most beautiful doll, came to class wearing a white fur cape over her sequined taffeta dress. Always on the lookout for photo opportunities, she never squirmed, never changed the royal tilt of her head. She was named after the British princess.

Shy elephant wouldn't speak, no matter how I coaxed. Panda, on the other hand, was a know-it-all. He folded his arms across his chest and, his beady eyes flashing with skepticism, refused to learn anything new. Diana wanted to turn every class into a party. She wore her skating costume to school, bare midriff and all.

Raggedy Andy lived in dreams. He never heard a word about homonyms: he wanted to know if cloud castles had plumbing or if fairies knew better than to eat poison mushrooms. Baby was always hungry. If her bottle fell out of her mouth, she wailed. She raised her hand only to ask if it was snack time.

Mr. Bear arrived late. He tossed spit balls at Margaret Rose. He burped in the middle of lectures. He told silly jokes about his family and then laughed and laughed until I had to scold him and put him in the corner. Class was dull while he was in the corner, so I always rescued him after a few minutes.

"Your play school is so-o-o loud," my mother would say.

"My students are so-o-o naughty," I'd tell her. "Teaching is hard work."

Today, I teach people, not dolls. But not much has changed. In the first class of the term, my students introduce themselves. Lily Ann tells us that after three months of writing, she's finally finished her thousand-page historical romance. "I expect to be on Oprah," she says. Sequins glitter on her cuffs and collar.

Patrick crosses his arms over his chest and tells us he has written sketches for more than fifty short stories. "Don't bore us with lectures," he says. "We know all that stuff."

Darlene flutters impossibly long eyelashes at Alan, the widower. She raises her hand and her leather top rises as well, revealing a tanned midriff. "Let's end class early," she says. "We can line dance till midnight at the Firebrand Lounge." She's going to be disappointed in Alan, I think: he truly lives in another world. He's writing a novel about a feminist James Bond. I call him Andy by mistake.

Gabriela slides into a chair at the back of the room. "Join us in the circle," I urge. She shakes her head and bends over her notebook. I think of shy Elephant and quickly call on Martha.

"I've written a cookbook," Martha says, enunciating with difficulty around what appears to be a large lemon drop. "One Thousand Ways to Prepare Formula for your Fussy Infant." She's brought her manuscript. Bottles wearing tiny bootees dance across each page.

Everyone is here, I think, except for Mr. Bear. Thank goodness for small favors. However, as we settle down after introductions, a man in brown sweats jogs through the door. "Sorry I'm late," he tells us while trying to catch his breath. "Stuff going on at home today. My boy got thrown out of fourth grade. My girl won the broad jump. After that, my printer jammed up." He stops to breathe and flourishes wrinkled papers at us. "I think all the sex scenes overheated the printer. Ha, ha, ha." He finally sits down and opens his notebook.

"Let's talk about character," I say, and in my voice I hear the excitement of a new class and new challenges. Now that Mr. Bear is here, we can begin

The author's graduation photo

I See Her So Beautiful

Awards: 3rd Place Pacific Northwest Writer's Conference (July 1992).

My daughter Rebecca is going to marry Christopher, a nice young man.

So my mother decides to plan the wedding. Pushing 85, you'd think she'd be ready to rest. But she keeps calling me from her home in Syracuse.

"I see her so beautiful in your wedding dress," she says. "It's perfect for her."

My mother is right. Ivory satin with Rebecca's strawberry blonde hair and deep healthy tan. "Great idea, Mother."

After we say goodbye, I dab more sunlight into my latest watercolor. As I paint, I dream about weddings—formal, informal, indoor, outdoor. Funny ones. Bizarre ones. Then I swish brushes in water and call Tulsa where Christopher and Rebecca have lived happily for three years.

"Mom!" Her voice is warm.

"I miss you," I tell her.

"We miss you and we miss Oregon," Rebecca says. "We hallucinate about Oregon. We've decided the wedding will be in the most beautiful place we can think of. In an Oregon old growth forest."

I smile. I can see it! The majestic trees, centuries old. The ferns. A natural cathedral. Perfect.

I tell her about my dress and how beautiful it will be on her.

"Ivory satin?" Her voice fills with doubt. "In the woods?"

"Maybe not," I answer. We switch our conversation to Christopher's troubles with his major professor. She tells me you can smell oil wells when the wind blows a certain way. We hang up.

The next time Mother calls, it's about the reception. "I found Aunt Mabel's recipe for ribbon sandwiches," she says. "They'll be so pretty on silver trays. Plus cherry bourbon fruitcakes wrapped in ivory lace."

In my mind, the silver trays rest on chiffon-draped tables. The reception area is bordered with arbors that bend under old-fashioned red roses. Our friends toast Rebecca and Christopher with sparkling burgundy in fluted goblets.

She's wearing my dress after all. And she's beautiful.

I call Rebecca. I tell her about the ribbon sandwiches and the fruitcakes. "I see baskets overflowing with forget-me-nots. I hear a harpsichord..."

"I'm not sure," she cuts in. "I'll talk to Christopher." Her voice sounds hurried. We hang up.

My mother calls the following week when I'm folding and stapling Art Guild newsletters. It's snowing in Syracuse. Mother can't go out. One good thing, the old growth idea takes her mind off the weather. She hates the old growth idea.

"Think of this wedding as a wonderful gift from you to her," she says. "A nice wedding. Your beautiful dress. In a church."

I staple two newsletters, then push the stapler aside. "She doesn't want a church wedding, Mother."

"Anne," she says. "Her wedding should be nice. Assert yourself."

We hang up. Assertively, I staple 150 newsletters. Then I call Rebecca. "Let's talk about something more traditional," I say. "Let's even talk about a church instead of the old growth."

"I don't think so," Rebecca says. "I'm late to work. Call you later?"

I stay away from the phone, determined to let her call me first. The following Saturday, she finally calls.

"It's sunny here," she says. "People are out on the golf course. We've been planning the wedding," she continues. "We want to write our own vows. We love each other so much. We want to say so in front of everyone."

A lump forms in my throat. I see them clasp hands, look into each other's eyes. They speak the words we all should have said. They make promises that will sustain them through the years ahead.

"We want the reception to be informal." Her voice is calm and full of certainty. "Salmon barbecue. Steamed clams. Garlic bread and strawberries." Pause. "White paper plates."

The silver trays fly out of the picture, tossed aloft like Frisbees. Rose-covered arbors tumble. Our friends, dressed in shorts and plaid shirts stand around picnic tables covered with blue checkered cloths. Barbecue smoke wafts across the clearing, carrying aromas of fish and garlic. Rebecca stands beyond the smoke. She's wearing my dress. She's eating potato salad. A bit of pickle falls from her fork and rolls down the front of the ivory satin.

"You probably don't want the harpsichord," I say.

"A marimba band."

"Nice," I tell her. We hang up.

In Syracuse, my mother says the roads are icing over and the Thruway's had eighteen accidents since five-thirty.

"About the wedding," I say. "I just talked with Rebecca."

"Why doesn't she let YOU plan it?" she asks. "Mothers have always planned weddings."

"You certainly planned mine." I suddenly remember how I had wanted my cake to be chocolate. My hair in bangs instead of combed back. I thread my fingers into the phone cord and then tug them out. "What about your mother? Did she plan yours?"

She goes back in time. Finally, she chuckles. "I wanted hydrangeas. I wanted my dress to be lavender. I wanted…"

She flies forward through sixty years and lands back into today. "But my wedding was fine. Mothers do know!"

"But what about your dream?" I ask. "What about the hydrangeas?"

She is silent. "Pink roses," she says. "Lots of pink roses. But I didn't know as much then," she says. "It turned out fine." I think her voice is not as strong.

"I'm going to let Rebecca have her dream," I say. I smile. Let her, indeed.

My mother starts to cry. "I only want her day to be perfect." Her voice wobbles and I recall with amazement how old she is.

I wipe my eyes, and all at once I know what to say. "We all want the same thing. A perfect day."

"Yes, we do." She blows her nose and comes back to the phone. "All right," she says.

At last. She lets go of Rebecca's wedding. And so, I let go too.

"They predict below zero tonight," she says.

"I can't imagine it. Don't go out, Mother. If you need anything, call someone."

"I have everything right here," she says. She pauses. "Just one question."

I cradle the phone under my chin and reach for my grocery list. Only four o'clock here in Oregon, and I have nothing worse than rain to deal with. I can stop thinking about Rebecca's wedding. Run some errands and.... "Yes, Mother?"

"I'm just asking...but, can't you...?"

I know what she's going to say. The grocery list crumples between my fingers.

"Try to change her mind about the dress," she says. "I see her so beautiful..."

The author's daughter (Rebecca Smith) and her husband
(Christopher Dymond) on their wedding day.

Adirondack Sun Porches

Published as "Those Sun Porches Warm Me Still." *Christian Science Monitor* 19 Mar. 2001: 18.

No matter where I go, I carry words from old songs and the smell of wood smoke from a long-ago campfire. I recall the warm moment of holding a newborn puppy and the dark, silent moment of a missed opportunity. Some of these memories lie sleeping; others are forever poking up their heads, begging to be noticed—the trivial tucked in with the momentous.

Naturally, my bundles of memories hold the faces and voices of my parents, my teachers, and my friends. But it seems to me I also carry topography—especially the soft contours of the Adirondack Mountains where I grew up. I carry that old house on Amherst Avenue in Ticonderoga. I even transport four sun porches.

I remember winter and how, in upstate New York, it backed off in slow, slow steps. First, perfectly good ice rotted on the lakes and ended our skating. Icicles, dangling from the eaves, once ripe for picking, wasted away. Along our street, as the sugar maples hinted green, our mothers hosed gritty sand off the sidewalks just in time for roller-skating. The dads no longer shoveled coal into furnaces in the morning. The radiators quit gasping and hissing; they held magazines instead of wet scarves and mittens.

And I remember how spring danced like a surprise into the corners of our house, into rooms that for months had known only artificial light. This dancing light came from the sun porch off the living room, a porch sealed away all winter behind curtained double doors lined with furry weather stripping. Those doors were closed so tight it took both my parents to jar them loose.

As the doors burst open, the light flew in. It carried smells of crocuses and mud—smells that overpowered the cellar scents of drying laundry, dusty coal, and a few winey McIntosh apples.

After that, another sun porch—the one off the kitchen - awaited its grand opening.

When that happened, it became a kind of greenhouse stacked with trays of tiny seedlings. Lilacs sent perfume by way of the sun porch into the kitchen. The geraniums on the windowsill sprouted buds.

Sun porches! In a land of freezing winters! What had the architect been thinking? As if two porches weren't frivolous enough, the upstairs had two more—useless all winter and all but forgotten until their doors were wrested open in the spring.

Their painted floors sloped like the decks of ships. Their drafty windows swung inward, like small

French doors, poised to brain the person foolish enough to bend under them.

The sun porch off my parents' bedroom held a creaky, metal bed covered with an orange and white hand-loomed bedspread. I slept there once or twice when company took over my room. Lying in that bed, with rough, shingled walls on one side and open windows on the other, I felt daringly exposed to thunderstorms and wild animals that I figured could easily leap to the second story.

The fourth sun porch opened off my bedroom. It was mine. I swung every window open, remembering, most of the time, not to bend under them. From my bed, I listened to early-morning pigeon melodies. At night, I sometimes heard the drone of an airplane, unusual in upstate New York at the time. The newly opened sun porches relaxed the stultifying rules of winter. They promised endless hours for imagining cloud shapes into stories or dancing with fireflies on the lawn.

I've carried my bundles of memories thousands of miles by now, stuffing in new images as I go. The sun porches ride alongside the flash of dolphins in a fiord, whistler swans gliding over a beach that glows with moonstones, a child forming her handprint in plaster of paris, the trusting eyes of an old dog.

But those Adirondack sun porches exert great power—they're stronger than you'd expect. They account for my odd behavior in March when I throw open doors and windows, insanely soon for the Adirondacks and too soon even here in the Pacific Northwest. Chill breezes spill across my bed from open windows.

My writing desk abuts the window sill in my office, never mind that the electric outlets are across the room. The trills of a house finch pipe me outside, where I linger to watch the breeze carve ruffles in the sequoias.

At night, as I gaze at my Oregon stars, fireflies sparkle again under the maples on Amherst Avenue.

My sun-porch memories sometimes nag. "Isn't it time for winter to back off?" They ask this even in the middle of summer. If I don't listen, they continue. "You've been closed up too long," they whisper again and again.

At last, I get it. Those bursting-open doors nag me to bend some rules, look outside myself. Let in new light. At those times, my sun porches ride atop my bundles of memories. Mine to carry—with joy.

A joyful Anne dances

Memory in a
Wicker Basket

Award: Honorable Mention 75th Annual Writer's Digest
Writing Competition (2006).

Sunday noon, Labor Day Weekend, and the family's reunion is in full swing in Springdale, Arkansas. To give my brother a break from mother care, I chose not to go to Springdale. Instead I came to Minnesota to stay with Mother in the "memory care" wing.

This morning, she and I had breakfast, did the dishes, and now she's sitting in her blue chair. I touch her arm and lean close. She opens her eyes and smiles. I tell her the news about my Jerry, that he loves working in his wood shop now that he's retired. I tell her how one day he was turning a huge wall platter. My arms form a circle to show how large. "The platter got loose from the lathe and flew past his head, up to the ceiling." My arms whoosh up. "It crashed into the fluorescent light, and then," I pretend to duck here, "he had wood and glass falling all around him."

Her face stays the same. Silence. "That's really something," she says softly.

I smile at her, but I'm tired. Those three

words—today's standard response.

Her stories, long and boring, used to trap me in her kitchen, in the bedroom, or halfway up the stairs on my way to the bathroom. Years ago, when her nouns disappeared, I got good at supplying the name, the place, the people, or even the whole point of her stories—not hard to do, since she told them over and over.

After the nouns, the verbs went away. But still she'd stop me on my way to get a glass of water or in the middle of a good chapter. I'd nod and nod. "Uh huh," I'd say.

When Dad was alive, he would bark, "Get to the point, Laura," but I could never get away with that. His stories made sense and were interesting. Hers, on the other hand, made fun or criticized. She told how annoying it was in Greece where so many people didn't even know how to "talk" English. She told us Hillary Clinton should stay home and be a wife. She said my daughters were out of control, and it was all my fault.

I touch her arm again. This time, she gets a dog story about how we left our yellow lab for a week at my daughter Rebecca's house. Her dog, Dune, and our Lucy turned naughty. "Guess what those dogs did?"

A long pause but something sparkles in her eyes.

"They stole a big hunk of cheese off the kitchen counter and ate it. Rebecca was disgusted."

Mother laughs. I wonder if she remembers how hard she always was on Rebecca, especially when she was a young mom. "You're just spoiling her," she scolded while Rebecca kissed the tears of her four-year-old Sierra. And then, as if she really believed it: "My own children never cried."

"Remember Whisky?" I ask. Mother's face goes blank. She doesn't remember the dog we had for fifteen years. "Rebecca was disgusted," I say, repeating the line that was successful.

What goes on inside her mind? Do fragments fly across too fast for her to catch? Does she see fleeting pictures of our house in Ticonderoga? Her own mother? The Christmas plum pudding? Or is it gray in there, a thick mist of nothing at all?

I move to sit by the window. People in shorts and sleeveless shirts cross the parking lot. A breeze moves through the leaves in the little maple tree that has grown a couple of feet each year Mother's been here. I yearn to be out there with people who can still stride out, swing their arms.

Visiting my mother has never been a reunion; I mean, nothing ever felt like a coming together. Before every trip, I would tell myself this time would be different. I'd vow she would not tear me apart. My purse held lists of things to do: ask her how it was when she was a child, get out the old photos, restring pearls, repot house plants. We did projects, but we never shared ideas. Mostly, I never spoke at all. I listened.

And now, here am I, bringing my own stories to the table.

One of the things we like to do here is cook breakfast together as we did this morning. Mother, in her wheelchair beside me in the small kitchen, helps me decide whether enough blueberries are in the batter. I let her tell me if it's time to turn the pancakes in the pan. I wheel her to the table with its blue and white place mats and help her set out the butter plate and syrup pitcher. Back in the kitchen I pile steaming pancakes onto a plate, put it in her lap, and push her again to the table. I remind her what to do with the butter and tuck a double napkin under her chin.

I'm learning to be careful with her. She had trouble with the orange juice this morning, just after I'd made such a show of shaking the carton, as if I was shaking a cocktail, and poured it with a flourish into a fancy glass. We toasted, and then she choked, and her eyes got wide and frightened.

"I made it too strong for you," I quipped and raised her thin arms till she stopped coughing. She's declined since June, the last time I saw her.

Now that breakfast is over, the day yawns before me. There is my book, my knitting, my stack of student papers, and in the parking lot is Janice's car for me to use while she and my brother Jack are in Arkansas. The family reunion is in its second day. The photos will have empty spaces; Mother and I won't be in them.

She might enjoy going for a ride but getting her in and out of the car takes all her energy, and mine. I could take her out in her wheelchair. Wouldn't she like to feel the breeze and the warm sun on her head?

The idea grows. A picnic. Outside under that maple tree. I swing about to tell her, but now she's dozing in the blue chair, her back curved, her neck crooked. I'll tell her when she wakes. Will she know what I'm talking about? Will "picnic" spark a connection after all these years?

In her bare-bones kitchen I find peanut butter and currant jelly. Half a loaf of bread in the freezer. A bunch of grapes. I see the paper napkins on the counter, and suddenly I know we have everything.

Something about paper napkins...

As I spread peanut butter on bread, I remember our Ticonderoga kitchen when I was a child. Blue linoleum, the red trestle table, geraniums on the window sill. The wicker picnic basket would be out, its lids flopped open. Mother putting in sandwiches of bologna, mustard, and Velveeta cheese. Chocolate chip cookies and apples. She stood a quart bottle of milk carefully in the basket. She put in the plates, cups, and napkins—all made of paper!

These days, we're used to paper plates and cups and napkins but back then, they were a luxury, used only for picnics. Those sweet cups nested into each other and blue flowers wound around their sides. The milk tasted different in them, and if you scraped one with your fingernail, a bit of wax would ruffle up.

Our picnics were spur-of-the-moment, because Dad would have phoned that he'd be home early from the mill that afternoon. It looked like a good evening to go out to the lake.

I can never describe a place the way I think it deserves. The trees, the Adirondacks, and Lake George were there; that's all I can say about them. If I were to go today to Ticonderoga, however, I could lead you to our picnic place. Up Amherst Avenue with its lines of sugar maples. Turn onto Black Point Road and drive south past homes with wide lawns that led down to docks and rowboats on the inlet. Pass the Vickers house and watch for Kate or Stan or one of their brown-and-white spaniels. Pass the Boffinger place, groomed and rich, people we didn't know—summer people—but every girl in town was in love with the "Boffinger Boys." Finally, turn right and go out to the Point.

For those long-ago picnics, I rode in the back seat and dangled one arm out the car window and the other across the picnic basket on the seat between me and Jack. It was early evening by then, and Black Point Beach was practically deserted, the swimmers gone home.

Mother and Dad would spread a thick felted blanket on the cushion of sand, and the blanket would become our chairs and table, our dining room, our entire home. Mother, sitting with stockinged legs curled under her, in her cotton dress and a small scarf over her hair, handed us sandwiches that crackled in waxed paper.

Ants and tickly things crawled on the blanket under my bare legs. Whitecaps danced on the lake, but closer in, water lapped and nuzzled the sand. Clouds raced across the sky and changed to pink, then orange, then gray. Close to us, much closer than when we were in town, the Adirondacks grew taller and loomed purple. Swallows and bats careened across the water. I remember Mother calling Dad "Hon," and he calling her "Kitty," and I cannot remember now when those names disappeared along with their love for each other.

Here in Mother's Minnesota apartment, there's no wicker hamper and no waxed paper. I slip the sandwiches into plastic bags, and add some grapes. I walk Mother to the bathroom, and get her seated in her wheelchair. I gather my sunglasses, her sun hat, a sweater. I never know when she'll be cold; her internal temperature no longer makes sense.

"We're going on a picnic," I tell her, and her face lights up. Is she responding to the word, or to the tone of my voice? I can't tell.

I hold up the plastic bag. "You hold our lunch," I tell her. Her face gets even more excited. Her hands meet mine as she gently cups them around the bag.

I push the wheelchair down the long hall and through the Great Room where the other residents have gathered. Some of them look up as we wheel through. "Hi, Wayne," I say. "Hi, Roger." "Hi, Bonnie."

As usual, Wayne stays silent, but Bonnie says, "Hello, there." Roger grins at us.

The aide is setting out chicken casseroles. "We're going out for a picnic," I tell her.

"Have a great time," she says, and fastens a bib around Wayne's neck.

The old ones look down at their plates. Do they remember crowding around a wicker hamper? Did they pull out sandwiches, each one wrapped like a gift? Did they wrinkle their noses at the taste of milk in a waxy paper cup? Do words like "picnic" contain so many tastes and sounds and smells that they forever keep their meaning?

As I punch in the code and wait for the lock to click open, Mother faces forward, her neck straight, her back solid. Taller than usual in her chair.

The author's parents, swimming in Lake George,
shortly after their marriage

*The author's parents visiting the author
in North Carolina shortly after the birth of their first
grandchild, her older daughter*

In the Tradition of Tulips

Tiny Lights, A Journal of Personal Narrative 10.1 (2004).

Awards: 2nd Place CNW/FFWA Florida State Writing Competition (2005); 2nd Place Tiny Lights Essay Contest (2004); 4th Place 72nd Annual Writer's Digest Writing Competition (2003); Top Ten finalist Pacific Northwest Writers Association Literary Contest (2000).

A big part of my job at Oregon State University's music department was cranking out enthusiastic press releases. That January day, with three months of a music festival stretching before me, I'd written seven of them. I printed the last one and checked my e-mail, happy to see respite from work—a note from my daughter Amy.

Amy lived in Ithaca, New York, much too far away. "Last night we got engaged," her e-mail said. "I'm so happy I can hardly breathe. The wedding will be in five months, in early May."

My mood changed. I moved the cursor toward "delete." A wedding? How could they? She and Sharon were a wonderful couple. But lesbians didn't get engaged. Didn't get married. Did they?

Of course, I couldn't delete it. I hit "reply." "I'm so happy for you," I wrote. "You know how I like Sharon. It's a great idea to celebrate your friendship."

Presto! "Wedding" had turned into "celebration of friendship." That worked for me.

Over the next months, however, Amy's e-mails and phone calls continued in the same vein. They'd chosen periwinkle silk for their dresses. They'd selected a flower girl and other attendants. They'd registered for gifts. I mumbled words of encouragement. The rest of the time, since they were so far away, I didn't think about "weddings" at all.

One evening in February, the phone rang. "We're finalizing the guest list," Amy told me. "Our limit is 150 people." As I suddenly thought of my mother I sagged into a chair and pulled a pillow into my lap. Almost ninety, Daughters of the American Revolution, Republican, Westchester County—my mother was going to be scandalized. "We have to leave Mother out," I said.

"I expected that," Amy said.

"But we can't," I said in the next breath. "If there's a family gathering that doesn't include her, she'll be furious."

Besides my mother, there was her brother, a former Presbyterian minister. Plus my own brother and his family. Amy's dad's family. "Couldn't you call it a celebration of friendship?" I asked. "They might go for that." I certainly had.

"It's a wedding, Mom," she answered. "With a minister. In the church."

I hugged the pillow against my chest. Why couldn't I enter into this?

A week later, Mother called. Her voice sounded like she'd discovered something dead under the refrigerator. "What's this about?" she asked.

I forced a laugh. "It's going to be a good party," I told her. "They've found a great band for the reception."

"What is this about?" she repeated.

I drew a deep breath. "They are a committed couple," I answered. "They want to make their commitment public. Everyone else does."

"Who did they send these things to?" she asked.

I told her who. "They didn't know what to do about your brother," I said. "Should they send him one?" She thought a moment. "Yes, they should," she said. I shook my head in disbelief. My mother could still surprise me.

In the meantime, Amy's sister was locating fabric and offering to sew the dress for the flower girl. I began to feel left out. I was the mom who'd always joined into the planning of birthday parties, backyard carnivals, Campfire Girl outings, all-night graduation-party breakfasts. Surely, I could help with this celebration. Er, wedding.

I phoned Amy. "I want to help," I said. "Maybe with the flowers?"

"That's a relief," she answered. "Thirty-five tables at the reception will need centerpieces."

"How about little vases of spring flowers?" I asked.

"Perfect," she answered. "Can you come early? We'll choose the flowers when you get here."

In the following weeks, we discussed reception halls, menus, and contracts with the band. I sewed the junior bridesmaid's dress and researched flower girl baskets. The details kept me from thinking.

A week before the wedding, I flew to upstate New York. Amy and Sharon's living room was hidden under boxes of votive candles, loops of artificial ivy, and bolts of periwinkle tulle. Wedding gifts stood in heaps next to the dining room table. Thank-you notes, ready to mail, mingled with lists on yellow tablet paper. This wedding was actually going to happen. I took a deep breath and picked up the yellow sheet that said "Mom." "Decide the flowers" was the first line.

"Did you know my family is Dutch?" Sharon asked me. "My mother loved tulips. We want tulips on the tables." Her face held the wistful expression I saw whenever she spoke of her mother who had died while Sharon was in college.

"I pictured wild irises," I said. "Forsythia and little daisies." Unreasonable stage fright filled my chest. "Tulips don't arrange. They droop."

"Traditions are a big part of this ceremony," Amy said. "The flower girl is going to scatter bay leaves; that's a Slovak tradition for Dad's side. We think the reception should have tulips for Sharon's."

They sat together at the table, their faces glowing. I told myself to love them more and stop thinking so much. But I well knew that a tulip once it's cut develops a mind of its own. I imagined thirty-five vases holding 175 independent-minded tulips.

Amy's other grandmother had said, "I don't understand her choice, but I love her. I'll be there." In fact, she was going to stand in for Amy's dad who couldn't attend since his wife was ill. My own mother had a different concern. "I'm afraid they'll lose their jobs," she'd confided. "Why can't they be quiet about this?"

All around me the gifts, the lists, the thank-you notes rebuked my doubts, my mother's doubts. "Did you ever hear from Uncle George?" I asked.

"He sent beautiful bath towels," Amy said. "And this letter." She handed it to me.

In eloquent ministerial language, my uncle had written about how families love and support their children. And how the God he believed in accepts all unions. Tears filled my eyes. I didn't know my uncle very well. Suddenly, I loved him.

Later that day, we went to see their church, a tradition in itself with rough-hewn stone and tall columns and stained glass, smells of candle wax and old hymnals. Amy handed me a church bulletin. When she pointed out the announcement of their wedding, my fears returned. Did the church members really approve? Would demonstrators come? Would someone shout something and stop the ceremony?

The next day, Thursday, Amy's sister arrived with the flower girl's dress in her suitcase. The same day, accompanied by their minister, Amy and Sharon went to City Hall. "They wouldn't give us a wedding license, so we filed a complaint," Amy said when they returned.

"Are you disappointed?" I asked.

"We expected it," Sharon told me. "But it was important to try."

We turned our attention to neckties for the ushers and earrings to match the periwinkle blue, but through it all, the problem of the tulips haunted me. In a burst of floral genius, I proposed adding apple blossoms that we could cut from the trees that had just burst into bloom. I figured apple blossoms would support the tulips. Amy and Sharon said that would be fine.

All at once it was Thursday night. With the wedding less than two days away, nothing was on schedule. The seamstress hadn't held the next-to-final fittings. Wasn't it time for FINAL fittings? The church program was mere words on Sharon's computer screen. Why couldn't they just print it out?

Things are always late at weddings, I thought. Why should this one be different?

On Friday, I filled the dining room table with vases, tulips, apple blossoms, and periwinkle tulle. Amy's sister and I worked together, inhaling scents of apple blossoms, fussing with the wimpy tulip stems. Thirty-five vases later, we moved on to corsages and boutonnieres and finished them off with tufts of periwinkle tulle. We sent the vases and corsages to stay overnight in coolers.

Relatives from both sides stopped in on their way to motels. We spoke of traffic jams, new construction, the weather. I studied their faces. What were they really thinking? I couldn't tell. All I knew was they'd made the trip. They'd be at the wedding.

The rings arrived. The seamstress promised to work all night. Someone printed out the program. But then, things went wrong again: The harpist phoned from O'Hare to report his plane was delayed. He'd miss the rehearsal. Always something, we groaned.

The whole time, my mind kept skipping through Amy's life, as if in a series of photos: Amy, three years old, playing in the sandbox, wearing her pink sundress. Amy, sixteen, dressed for the prom in an emerald gown, her beautiful red hair fastened up with white camellias. Amy's letter, the one she sent us from college, telling us she was a lesbian. I was undone by that letter. I grieved that her life would be harder than it should be. Like this wedding. How would it go? How would we remember it?

On Saturday, the big day, we gathered in the old sanctuary. The photographer grouped and regrouped us. I pinned on corsages and met more people who would be Amy's new relatives. Amy and Sharon floated through it all, wearing lipstick and blusher, elegant and graceful in periwinkle silk.

Finally, it was time for those of us who would be in the processional to go upstairs, to wait for the signal. Below us, we heard the sounds of people arriving. I looked out a front window, pretending to check the weather, really checking for hate signs, for demonstrators. I saw none. Downstairs in the sanctuary, a lilting Irish tune began, the harpist playing beautifully in spite of being up all night.

The harp music ended and the African drums began. I followed the drummers down the aisle, carrying one special vase of tulips to place beside the photo of Sharon's mother. As I turned around, I realized that every pew was filled. I saw my brother from Minnesota, my nieces and nephews. My mother. Aunts, uncles, cousins from both sides—Sharon's and Amy's. The others were their friends from church, from work, from drumming groups.

As I took my place, the flower girl scattered her bay leaves. Amy and Sharon, looking radiant and beautiful, followed her down the aisle. The drums stopped.

We stood in silence as the minister stepped forward and raised her arms, her long sleeves spread at her sides like angel wings. She invited us to give Amy and Sharon our love and to bless this marriage. The traditions that followed were drawn from every branch of family and friends. Sharon's Aunt Karen sang "Ave Maria," her sweet voice soaring into the rafters of the old church. Amy and Sharon spoke of their commitment to each other and exchanged their rings. They signed a ketubah to publicize their commitments, a Jewish tradition. Amy's sister bound the couple's wrists with a golden cord, performing the Pagan tradition of "handfasting."

Amy and Sharon kissed and hugged and ducked through an archway made of apple blossoms. As they went up the aisle, in a final tour de force, they "jumped the broom" in honor of black slaves who had once celebrated their unions in this way since they too were forbidden to marry. At that, we couldn't help ourselves: we applauded and cheered in a most unchurchly way. Recalling where we were, we wiped our eyes, blew our noses, grinned crooked grins. We reached for the hands of our own loved ones.

Beside me, my mother tucked a damp tissue into her sleeve.

I'd stopped worrying about the tulips. As we entered the reception hall however, I saw that, just as I'd feared, some tulips had turned to stare at the windows; some tulips had bent over to touch the tablecloths. Not one vase looked like any other.

All that work.

But then. I had to admire the delicacy of those arched stems. I noticed how the petals belled into perfect cups. I remembered that they were, after all, a gift from the mothers—from me and from Sharon's mother.

Tulips, I thought, are like children. They sometimes turn in directions we might not choose for them.

They are still beautiful.

The author's daughter (Amy Beltaine)
and Sharon Beltaine, 1998

In Good Hands

Tiny Lights, A Journal of Personal Narrative 11.1 (2005).

We sprawled across the carpet of our new home, sore from lugging beds and dressers, clothes and books. Our furniture twitched around us like homeless teenagers hoping to fit in. We'd moved everything we owned—from his house and from mine.

Beside me, Jerry, the man I was creating a home with, stretched and groaned, a sound that echoed off the undecorated walls.

He waved his hand toward a stack of cardboard boxes, each labeled with one word: SILVER. "Weighed a ton," he said. "What's in them?"

"Baggage," I answered, and I heard the walls amplify a tremble in my voice.

"I don't want to see," he said.

"I don't want to show you."

He upended his bottle of beer, drank it down, and closed his eyes. His hand moved to grasp mine, and love tingled up my arm and into my heart. My Jerry was a potter, and potters brought magic. I'd known that for years.

My hunger for a potter's magic first surfaced when I was a child in upstate New York. My family took visitors first to Fort Ticonderoga where we'd gawk at muskets and climb the cannons that lined the ramparts. The second attraction was on the road back to town. If the potter was in his front yard working at his wheel, Dad would stop the car. We'd pile out.

Finished pots lined the porch steps and leaned against trees and bushes—strange places, I always thought, for storing dishes. The potter would nod and say hello before his foot kicked the wheel back up to speed. As he leaned into his work, I scrutinized his hands, thinking maybe this time, I'd see how he did the magic.

In the cup of his hands, the clay grew into a mound, shiny and brown as chocolate ice cream. My dad always stood beside me, unafraid of splatters, but Mother stayed back. As I watched the potter make something from nothing, I imagined my parents finally believing in possibilities. I imagined them turning in great surprise to ME! Delighted, after all, with me.

His hands shifted; the clay rose into a tower before he mashed it down. As his foot rhythmically thunked the fly wheel, the clay sides flared out; the piece turned hollow. His fingers moved again; the sides curved in. We hummed our pleasure. He nodded his reply.

He dipped fingertips into the bucket of water at his side and smoothed the top of what had become something elegant. Finally, he slowed the wheel and stopped it, lifted the piece to show us. There, I thought. THIS time, they'll see it.

But when I looked at my parents, they were the same.

I had set my table with hand-thrown pottery over the years, but I was too busy being a wife and mother to consider the hands that had shaped it. I was living in a small Oregon town, divorced and in my mid-forties, when I began a search for a tureen of a certain size and shape. The tureen, when I found it, was in a studio a few miles away. Naturally, the studio also held the potter.

The smell of wet clay and the sight of magical hands drew me close. I stayed to watch and talk. Later, he phoned me. Still later, we fell in love.

In the life I'd shaped since my divorce, pot-luck suppers and folk music jam sessions had taken the place of formal dinner parties. Jeans and flannel shirts had replaced my nylons and sweater sets. Writing filled the time I'd once spent mothering and homemaking.

Since Jerry and I were getting more and more serious, I called my parents to tell them. Predictably, they asked, "What does he do?"

"He's a potter," I answered, and wondered if they remembered the Ticonderoga potter. If they did, they didn't say. Instead, they worried that this man was different from my first husband. (That's the point, I thought.) On the other hand, they were sure I shouldn't be "running around loose." A husband would make me "respectable" again. But a potter? They feared he was too different from the family and from the people they spent time with. In Westchester County, their world ran according to commuter train schedules and market fluctuations.

I reached for words they could translate. "Fine galleries carry his pottery," I told them. "He's putting his kids through college. He does well." The translations? "Prestige," "Higher education," "Wealth."

"Ah," they said, some small relief in their voices. "Can we meet him?"

"Come visit," I answered, pleased I could still speak their language.

When they arrived, Jerry came for dinner. As lasagna steamed on the counter and I tossed a green salad in one of his blue-and-white porcelain bowls, they politely quizzed him. "Quitting my teaching job seemed crazy," he told them. "I had little kids back then. What was I thinking?" He paused. "I couldn't stay away from the potter's wheel," he said.

They were charmed by his candor. They admired the salad bowl, remembered the "fine galleries." They relaxed.

They've mellowed, I thought. I brewed coffee and breathed in family—old blending with new.

The next day, at his house, he served deli sandwiches and fresh strawberries. Mother and I lingered over coffee while Jerry took Dad on a studio tour. They came back smudged with clay dust, discussing chemicals and cone firings. As we got into my car, Dad squeezed my arm. "He's great," he said.

Mother was quiet.

"Well," she said, as she settled later on the couch at my house, "that was very interesting." She unrolled her needlework, a flowered tapestry, and tugged at the corners to square the canvas.

I moved around the room, watering house plants. In a few days, I mused, my parents would return home. But they were part of us now—the foundation for building my new family.

Her voice came again. "This won't work," she said. "He's not right for you."

Water burped out the spout of my brass watering can. I dropped a tissue over the puddle. Watched it soak up water.

"He has no furniture," she said. She eased a length of yarn from a blue skein and threaded her needle.

I pictured Jerry's furniture, a chunky style of Mediterranean. Blending my French Provincial with it was going to be a challenge. But, so?

"No NICE furniture," she added.

In a flash, it came to me. No antiques! She figured if nothing "of value" had come down through his family, his family probably had nothing worth passing on. That raised serious questions.   "He has plenty of furniture," I said, but my lips fumbled the words.

She jabbed her needle into the canvas. She knew she was right.

I pinched a brown leaf from the African violet and knocked off perfectly good leaves at the same time. She's preposterous, I thought. But in the kitchen, out of her sight, I cooled my forehead against the refrigerator door. Was she saying we were too different?

On the other hand, was I making a mistake? Was I bewitched by memories of magical potters?

Talking to Dad would do nothing. He always let Mother win the round; it was easier. So, the next day, I took them to see a dahlia farm. We went to the coast and to the mountains. Jerry's name never came up.

After they went home, doubts grew like a slow-moving infection. I noticed Jerry was often late. Was he not good at organizing his time? I noticed how he loved his baggy orange nylon shorts. Didn't he look in a mirror? I noticed cobwebs on his front porch. Didn't he care what people might think?

The foundation I craved had holes in it. Did all mothers have this power?

I ordered myself to "make a list." Two lists: the bad and the good. The "bad" took only a few minutes; the "good" took longer and had more clout. The ways we discussed our children. Our understanding of each other's work as we both turned raw materials into art—his clay on the wheel, my words on paper. The way he said, "I love you," and then nudged me to say it back to him—words I'd seldom said out loud.

Clout.

Eventually, my doubts dwindled. A few months later, he and I bought the house.

I touched his shoulder, hard muscle under the cotton tee-shirt, as he lay on the carpet in our new home. Then, something inside of me, the thing that never leaves well enough alone, prodded me. I tapped my fingers on one of the boxes. "We could look at it," I said.

He didn't move, but his breathing changed. He was listening.

I wrestled one box away from the others. The boxes held silver, but they might as well have held antiques and parents. But I've put that behind me, I thought.

Had I?

I undid the cardboard flaps and drew out a small package. "Ah," I said, "the wedding present of choice in 1959 on the East Coast."

He opened one eye, gazed at the silver candlesticks. Closed his eye.

"And here," I said, "are the candy dishes."

He grunted as I set the small dishes around his head. My fingers stroked a graceful pedestal as I recalled long-ago holiday dinners. Blue goblets, white linen, and candlelight that softened my mother's face.

The next box held a tea service. I placed a plump sugar bowl beside Jerry in his jeans and tee shirt, holding his empty bottle of beer. "When I was a faculty wife," I said, "ladies came for lunches." Did I hear wistfulness in my voice?

"I like you better now," he said, sitting up, looking revived. "What do you think? Shall we go roll around?"

"In a minute," I said. "One more box." I took out the serving dishes, removed their soft wrappings, and clanked their covers on. With a potter's interest, he turned them over, appraised their lines, assessed the fit of the covers.

"It's a culinary crime," I said. "Silver vegetable dishes suck heat from broccoli in split seconds." I drew a deep breath. "I'm done now."

He took my hand again and I felt how strong his fingers were. "Now I've seen them. Now what?"

I swallowed over the lump in my throat. "They're heavy," I said finally. "You get the whole package."

"These aren't you," he said, looking confused. "These are too shiny."

"I wish." I buried my face in his shoulder, and smelled the sweat from our day's work. "I come from a shiny family," I told him. "Especially, my mother."

As I breathed him into me, the grip of my parents loosened. He believes in possibilities, I remembered. He's a potter.

But...this potter didn't know everything. He didn't know the child who peeked into silver dishes that reflected back a huge nose and beady eyes. He didn't know the young wife who covered up unhappiness with glitter on the table. He was still getting to know the woman who'd taken charge and started shaping a different kind of life.

I hugged my knees against my chest. Today's woman knew a thing or two about families. Mostly, you built them from what you had inside.

The silver pieces glittered in this room. Out of place. "Let's pack these away," I said.

We wrapped the silver into flannel cloths. A few minutes later we had it packed again inside the cardboard boxes. Temporarily stacked against the bare walls, the boxes would do one good thing: they'd muffle the echoes—echoes from the past. My new family was building its foundation. Whatever materials we chose would be the kind that held heat.

Jerry in his studio

The Weight of a Hat

My mother sits across the room from me, in her blue chair. Under the lamp—always on because in summer the trees are thick and this house is always dark—her white hair glows. She stares at nothing as her hands clench and unclench. Her mouth forms a tight, straight line. A moment ago, she told me that Jack and I are crazy. Told me again she's not going anywhere.

Our plane leaves in three hours. I should be upstairs packing her bags.

Footsteps sound overhead; my brother Jack prowling the attic, both of us not daring to tell her the movers will pack up the contents of the house in three days. How will he sort everything for them? There's fifty years of stuff—camping gear from the Thirties, precious antiques, dented cookware, fine needlework.

Her minister came this morning. When he told me we are doing the right thing, I had to blink back sudden tears. We're not sure—not sure at all—that this move won't kill her. After all, this is her home. And she's 96!

"I'm not going anywhere," she told the minister. He looked at me in dismay.

"We hired a private plane," I whispered. "Jack's staying here to sort things. I'm going with her." A private plane, because we knew we'd never get Mother, angry and incontinent, through security at the public airport. Her minister talked with her about changes and fear. For a few minutes he had her almost agreeing. But that was this morning.

I arrived in Chappaqua two days ago: the trip a mixture of pain and relief. Relief, because I was never going to have to do this endless, uncomfortable flight again. I will not miss these narrow roads and the decrepit grocery stores with their overpriced produce and hostile clerks. I will not miss the pretentious mansions tended by Latino gardeners and nannies, or the humid, mosquito-driven summers.

My mind is also working on the same lists that fill my brother's head. The red brocade couch with its needlepointed pillows will go last into the moving van for the assisted living place, as will the china cabinet. The dining room table that has stood fifty years on that red wool rug is destined for storage. I will not miss that table and the memories of silent, tense meals choked down there.

"Jack found you a wonderful apartment in Minnesota," I tell her. "No stairs to climb." She doesn't look at me. "I'll stay a week with you. If we don't like the place, I'll take you back to Oregon with me."

She shudders.

"Wouldn't you like to pack your suitcase now?"

"Just stop it," she says. "I'm not going." Her glasses glitter at me. She reaches for the mail on the table beside her. She doesn't remember she's already read this mail.

On my way up the stairs, I hear my brother calling from the guestroom. "I need your opinion about these."

"I've got to pack for her," I say, but when I reach the end of the hall I see that he's surrounded by hat boxes.

He opens a box. We peer in. A hat, dark blue and oval, nestles in yellowed tissue paper. A gray feather curls out. He opens another to find a black straw pill box circled with pink rosebuds like on a decorated cake. He opens a smaller box to a fluff of feathers—periwinkle—and I remember Mother wearing this hat to a party at the Ticonderoga Country Club. Her dress, the same color, was noisy taffeta with a flounce at the hip. He's still opening boxes. The next one holds a black velvet cloche, shirred into tiny gathers, soft and luscious. Smells of Mother's face powder drift up.

She never crowded her hats. Each one nested in its own striped, flowered, or polka-dotted box. She believed that wearing the right hat would lead her to something better. Wealth? Prestige? Happiness? Hats were a big part of her plan to get out of a mill town.

"We can't store everything." I sit on the bed in despair. "Can we?"

"The attic is awful," he says. "Empty cardboard boxes. Old magazines. Cartons of old curtains." He sits on the edge of the bed, his shoulders slumping. "I have to go through everything. It looks like junk, but it might not be. There's also the basement."

I picture old kitchen chairs, stacks of flower pots, Dad's hunting and fishing gear, and garden supplies. "Good thing you ordered the biggest dumpster."

"The hats can't go in the dumpster," he says.

My throat closes. "We should have called an estate person for help, but how could we? Mother wouldn't have let her in." I open more boxes to the sheen of taffeta, the sparkle of beads, the luxury of fur. I wonder if my old hats are here.

For months, he and I have been facing this moment. As Mother repeatedly called 911 to report faces looking in her windows and noises in her attic, the police repeatedly called Jack to say she needed more supervision. We hired round-the-clock companions for her while we agonized over what to do. We found the assisted-living place near his Minnesota home. We chose the moving company, the private airplane, and the real estate agent who will sell this house. We selected what she might want in her new apartment—pieces of furniture, down to details that included her address book, subscriptions to her favorite magazines, and her African violets. Nothing we did is right because we had to guess. She thinks she's not going.

All this sorting of things, this sorting of emotions, will take years. My mother's things have defined our family. Each piece has a story. To her, each piece is priceless.

I run my fingers over labels on the hat boxes: Halston, Christian Dior, Sally Victor. Hats have always confused me; they have always sat too heavy on my head.

He looks again at his watch. "Do you want your ski jacket from eighth grade? It's next to her mink coat."

I turn to him. "Every closet is full of stuff like that. Toss whatever you want to." He looks over to see if I'm kidding. I swallow hard. "You have three days to make a thousand decisions. I'm trying to make it easier for you."

In Mother's bedroom, I fill suitcases with her skirts and sweaters, her nighties, her cosmetics, her alarm clock, my dad's photo. She's always done her own packing, and I'm sure I'm doing it wrong. My hands shake. My heart is breaking, and I picture them in the other room: Mother's hats. I know what they meant to her. I've sentenced them to death.

But there's another side. I see her in her hats: going to Garden Club meetings when I was little, presiding over a Daughters of the American Revolution meeting in Washington when I reached college, walking off planes and into airport waiting rooms after I moved to Oregon. My daughters always hoped for a soft grandma; instead they got my mother in a hat.

In 1948, to get to Miss Mullen's Millinery Shop, Mother and I had to walk down Amherst Avenue, go around the Catholic Church and down Champlain Avenue. As we went, the smell of the Ticonderoga paper mill grew stronger. The mill was the place where, according to Mother, Daddy went too often, every time the phone rang—even in the middle of the night.

That morning, Mother's flat toque and wisp of veiling matched the blue of her light wool coat. Women in those days wore feathered cloches to ladies' luncheons. They pulled on felt beehives for shopping and flower-trimmed straw hats for picnics. Children, as well. I got two new hats each year, felt for fall, straw for spring.

A silver bell over Miss Mullen's door tinkled as we entered, and our arrival stirred ribbons and laces to life. Smells of glue and damp wool filled my nose. Miss Mullen was in the back, bent over her big table that was cluttered with felt blanks, bolts of veiling, and shears with great, long blades. As she settled Mother into a chair in front of the mirrors, they chatted about New York City and Saks Fifth Avenue. They sighed about this mill town.

"Anyway," Mother said, "I had my hair done yesterday."

"It looks lovely," Miss Mullen said as she re-moved Mother's hat. And then, "I have set aside some hats just for you."

Because I was ten, I was allowed to wander the shop and try on a hat or two. My favorites were ones a movie star might wear; studded with rhinestones. They made me feel pretty.

When it was my turn to sit in the chair, Mother never had rhinestones in mind. "Try this," she'd say as she pushed something tight onto my head. She would step back just like Miss Mullen. "This hat will do it," she'd say, and suddenly heavy on my head was a dark, hot thing with a serviceable grosgrain ribbon. I knew from over-hearing late-night arguments that Mother wanted to move to a place where women understood that handbag and shoes should match, and that a hat was the finishing touch.

Miss Mullen would form her lips into an "ohhhh" while I stared at ugly me's in the three-way mirrors. With the help of this new hat, it was clear I was to grow up to be elegant and privileged. I was to fulfill my mother's dreams.

In 2000, fifty years later, when my mother was merely 94, my husband Jerry and I left our Oregon home to vacation in New Zealand. For four days, rain fell over the North Island. We put on our Oregon rain gear and toured Paihia and Russell by dodging from coffee shops to museums and back to coffee shops. On the fifth morning the skies cleared, and we reserved kayaks. We planned to paddle upriver to look for birds.

On our way back to the motel after breakfast, we passed a shop window filled with hats. I stopped. Gloom filled my chest.

"What's up?" Jerry asked.

"I need a hat for kayaking this afternoon." My forehead already prickled. My pale skin burns easily.

"You didn't bring a hat?" He pushed back his ball cap and stared at me. He loves hats. They keep him warm—something he tells me I'll never understand until I too am bald. "I'll meet you back at the motel," he said.

I pushed open the shop door, almost expecting to hear the tinkle of a silver bell. It was possibly the first real hat shop I'd been in since the days of Miss Mullen. I looked around, half expecting to see her put down her shears and walk toward me, but instead I saw that the far wall bristled with hats, most of them caps with visors. At one side I saw a rack of tulle concoctions for the refined person who might still dress for dinner. Rows of garden hats filled another wall. There was no Miss Mullen; this was a modern-day, serve-yourself hat shop.

I would grab the first hat that would protect me from sunburn, hand over the New Zealand bills, and catch up with Jerry.

I couldn't hurry at this. Hats were not reliable. When I was in eighth grade my pink straw hat had rubbed an ugly welt above my right eyebrow. My yellow linen hat clamped on like a vise and gave me headaches. In high school, the black triangle with the red feather turned me into a unicorn.

I had tried to rise to the expectations of the hats, but Mother remained disappointed even though I eventually left Ticonderoga and went to college. She was furious when I refused to join the Daughters of the American Revolution. She was devastated when I married a man who was only a professor, and alarmed when I moved to Oregon, a place where, she said, people barely knew how to set a formal table. She was appalled that I wrote books instead of being a proper wife and mother. She was disgusted by my choice. She said my getting a divorce had ruined my children.

An hour of my vacation trickled away while I tried on ball caps that lengthened my nose, boating hats that blinded me with floppy brims, straw hats that would fly off in the slightest breeze. Static electricity crackled through my hair as I pulled on a big, green linen garden hat. In it, I looked like Dopey.

My mother is here, I thought. On my vacation.

I could see her. We're ready to go somewhere, Daddy waiting in the car, and Mother frowning. "You don't have your hat."

"I don't need a hat." I start to sweat.

"You have a nice hat. Get it." Her own hat quivers as she crosses her arms and waits.

"The other kids won't have hats, Mother," my brother would say, "She's going to look weird!"

"The others don't know how important a hat is."

I shook Mother's voice away as I removed the Dopey hat. I reached for a blue thing with a long bill and a little skirt poking out the back. The bill would shade my nose; the skirt would protect my neck. The hat was so ugly, the whole store would look better if I took it away.

At the cash register, the man made change and small talk. "Visiting from the States?"

"We love your country. It's beautiful."

"This is a small town," he said, as if apologizing.

"Small towns are great." As I spoke I pictured home-made popsicles, and swimming in Lake George, raking maple leaves into huge piles before jumping into them, and ice skating inside the flooded high school baseball diamond. My mother's crossed arms faded away, along with Miss Mullen's Millinery Shop and smells of paper mill.

He pushed the blue hat across the counter. "Want a bag? Or will you wear it?"

Wear it? The old habits kicked in as my mother rejoined us. "It's for the river this afternoon."

He raised his eyebrows as if he didn't understand. I grabbed the hat, waved goodbye, and stepped out into the blazing sun. Carrying my hat.

Today, in the small Oregon town that I call home, I'm getting dressed before joining Jerry at the baseball game on campus. The game begins at 1:30 and, since it's a sunny June day, I pull on long sleeves, toss sun block into my tote bag, and then duck into the closet to peer up at my shelf of hats—a jumble of bicycle helmets, swim caps, ski hats, rain hats, and even the cowboy hat I wore to the Pendleton Roundup.

Mother would be scandalized by the way I keep my hats.

Two years have passed since we moved her from New York to Minnesota. When I last visited, she was in a hospital bed, sipping liquids from a spoon, fading in and out of sleep. I perched on the edge of her bed, played the guitar and sang to her as she smiled and nodded. She liked every photo I brought, every story I told. These days, my brother says in his phone calls that she sometimes doesn't recognize him. She wakes for a few minutes and he holds up an African violet to let her see the new buds. "That's beautiful," she says.

Did dementia erase her discontent? Maybe so. Or perhaps she rediscovered what I had always hoped for her: happiness comes from inside—not from a Dior label or the red brocade on an antique couch.

I fumble along the closet shelf and toss aside the awful New Zealand hat—still too ugly. The rodeo hat is covering a hat I'd forgotten—soft straw, sashed with a floppy tie-dye ribbon. Eye-catching. Where did this come from?

I remember a student in my writing class.

He thought he'd written the perfect murder mystery, based on his experiences as a golf pro. He brought golf caps with his club's logo stitched on them to the final class—a hat for each student. Then, beaming, he presented me with a special "teacher" hat: this bodacious wide-brimmed straw hat with its floppy bow. For some reason, he thought it suited me.

I jam it on, thinking I must get going if I'm to see the beginning of the game. I grab my tote and race for the car. In the mirror, as I tear past it, I glimpse a pretty woman.

A few minutes later, I walk the bleacher rows to find Jerry. I'm wearing the hat, and by then, I'm almost sure the pretty woman in the mirror must have been me. When I get to him, he pushes up his sunglasses and says, "Hey!"

I stay nonchalant.

"Where'd you get that hat?" he asks as I climb up and settle beside him.

"It was in the closet." I pull bagels out of the tote, hand him one.

He wraps one arm around me and nuzzles my ear. "Nice."

I imagine that back in Minnesota, Mother opens her eyes for a moment. "The right hat," She murmurs.

The hats. Whatever happened to them?

Whenever I thought about those days when Mother was so angry and when Jack and I faced the enormous task of sorting and packing and making a new home for her, I felt simple relief that we got through it.

Hats were the last thing on our minds as we worked to help Mother adjust to the new place. When her Chappaqua house sold, she understood she could never go back. She surprised us when she didn't seem concerned.

Whenever I happened to think of the hats, it was with deep sadness. They had been lovely, and they had held my mother's history. We should not have thrown them away. My brother's job that day was impossible, and I gave him permission to toss. Sure, we were overloaded, terrified that we were doing the wrong thing, badly needing her help. But still.

Mother lived to be 98. She grew to like her pretty apartment and the people who helped her through each day. She was happy to live closer to Jack. Glad to see me each time I visited.   Shortly after she died in 2005, Jack heard from a member of the Daughters of the American Revolution. Along with her condolences, she wrote: I wanted to share with you a fund-raising project tentatively scheduled for our 2006 State Conference. Many years ago it was most fashionable to wear hats, all the time, hats for all occasions. We thought we could run a silent auction of hats from some of the past Regents if we could gather enough of them. If there are some hats that your mother had and that you can bear to part with, we would love to display and offer them for sale. The proceeds would benefit the project of the current State Regent.

"This makes it worse," I e-mailed Jack. "We threw away those hats. I'm so sad."

"Don't feel bad," he wrote back. "They ended up in our attic."

I was furious that he hadn't let me know sooner. I called him. "What do you think?" I asked. "Shall we give some hats to the DAR?"

"I'll pick through them, find some good ones. Do you want any?"

Suddenly, I did. "Could you send the little one that is made of feathers? Blue?"

He laughed. "Sure," he said.

We were quiet a moment.

"Mother would be pleased about her hats going to the DAR," I told him. "She would say... What did she used to say? She'd say 'This hat will do it.'"

"Hmm," he said. He was not remembering what I remembered. But then, he never went to Miss Mullen's.

Dressing the Emperor

By the time I get to my stopover in Chicago, the clothes that made me feel pretty back home in Oregon have become too casual. My sandals, the batik tote bag, and my softly gathered cotton skirt mark me as "west coast." The leather-heeled, pant-suited women waiting with me for the plane to Westchester County carry assertive handbags and operate cell phones with fingers that could star in Revlon ads.

To keep from obsessing about this, I pull a notebook from my tote bag and open it to the list I've made for this visit with Mother. "Things We Can Do." "Visit the mansions" tops the list. They really are mansions, and they are growing like a small kingdom east of Mount Kisco. Like poor relatives, Mother and I will stare out the car windows at the columned porches and luxurious landscaping. We'll guess the number of bathrooms—six, seven, or maybe eight—and picture the nanny's room and the maid's room. Mother will see a house she prefers to the one she has. I'll wonder if the people living inside such a house can be happy, but I won't say that out loud.

As another costumed-for-success woman sits down beside me, I draw my offensive sandaled feet out of sight and return to the list. "Armonk Nursery." Pushing Mother's wheelchair along the gravel paths and into every greenhouse won't be easy, but the orchids and fancy begonias will charm us. We'll select fuchsia seedlings to make a hanging basket for her porch. The nursery employees will see a perfect mother and daughter. I draw a happy face next to "Armonk Nursery" and push the corners of my lips up to match.

By the time we line up for boarding, my optimism has evaporated again. This visit will be no different from all the others. She will contradict, instruct, correct. Why, after all these years, do I keep thinking anything might change?

Stand up straight, I tell myself, and there it is: In spite of myself I sound like my mother.

At the Westchester County Airport, the man hands me the keys to the rental car and, in accents out of Yonkers, directs me to the car lot. Fifteen minutes later, I'm driving down Mother's tree-lined street. The list in my head gains more entries: "Invite Dene, Mother's neighbor, for dinner." "Get out the photo albums." Mother will talk and talk about those pictures.

As I step out of the car, damp heat presses and oppresses. Cicadas chatter overhead, invisible in the dense green. I brush wrinkles out of my skirt that, at home, I thought was rich garnet but here, in Mother's driveway, is fire-engine red. My suitcase wheels catch on the flagstones that lead me to the porch.

This is when every visit falls into the same patterns. Mother will stand on the other side of the screen door, a blur of white hair and glasses, wearing a skirt and pretty cardigan, and then I'll pull open the door and step in. We'll do our usual hug, the one where our cheeks touch, and I'll smell the glycerine and rose water she pats onto her face each morning. She'll ask about my trip, but after two sentences from me, she'll no longer be interested.

I open the screen door, step in. She isn't there.

"I'm here," I call. No one answers.

Dark shadows fill the living room. Her blue chair looks recently sat in; she's been reading the mail. A glance into the kitchen tells me she's not there either. "Hello," I sing out and those damn everlasting hopes for a happy visit burst into my chest, make me gasp. By this time, Mother and I have white hair. We have lived the lives of daughters, mothers, and even grandmothers. Surely, this time we will have important things to say to each other.

It was the late Forties, and I was eight. Every Saturday, Mother said no I couldn't go to the matinees that featured Gene Autry (too violent?), but she allowed Esther Williams movies because of the graceful underwater ballets. When the Esther Williams paper doll book came out, I carried it home and carefully punched out the dolls. She came in two poses, which I named Esther and Elaine. I pretended they were twin sisters.

The curved legs on the coffee table in the living room made a perfect place to prop paper dolls. One wintry Saturday morning, Esther and Elaine were in the middle of a terrible argument when the doorbell rang. The problem, as I recall it, was that Elaine wanted to borrow Esther's green-and-purple silk evening dress. "Absolutely not!" Esther yelled. "You don't take care of things. You know you lost my diamond bracelet." The bracelet was indeed missing; I had looked through the piles of accessories several times and couldn't find it. When the doorbell rang again, I pulled myself back into the real world and went to answer it.

Standing on our front porch, Mrs. Chandler clutched a black purse against her chest and her tweed wool coat billowed around her legs. She stared at me, her eyes startled like a deer's eyes as I struggled to make sense of her coming. We didn't really know her.

"Come in," I finally said, and she stepped through the door as Mother came down the stairs.

"Mary," she said. "Come in out of the cold." Her frown at me made me realize I'd held the door open a long time. Mother had on heels and a dress she'd made, one with a white collar and a fabric belt. Her lipstick was bright; her eyebrows had been plucked into narrow lines.

"Oh," Mrs. Chandler said. "I came just as I was."

"I'm glad you could come at all." Mother took Mrs. Chandler's coat and then, Mrs. Chandler hugged her purse to her heavy wool sweater. She had on slacks and crepe-soled shoes.

"Play somewhere else, Anne," Mother said as she led Mrs. Chandler into the living room. As they stepped around Esther Williams and settled on the couch, they chatted about how thick the ice was on Lake Champlain and how someone's car had skidded into a telephone pole.

The dining room table legs weren't as good, but I took everything in there and settled down on the red rug. The trouble was, in this new setting Esther and Elaine had gone speechless. All I had were echoes of raised voices, passion about something important, and their whole relationship at risk.

My mother offered coffee and went to the kitchen. As she returned to the living room, Mrs. Chandler was blowing her nose, and Mother got up again to get her a fresh tissue.

"Hard for you," Mother's voice said.

"I'll be okay," Mrs. Chandler said. "I'll be fine."

I put Elaine into a blue dress that had a long train that she held up with a strap on her wrist. "That dress is very nice," Esther told her, but she was lying. We both knew Elaine, dressed in dull, ordinary blue, was going to stand in the corner while everyone else danced.

"Sugar?" Mother asked.

"Thank you." A spoon clicked against a coffee cup.

Mother cleared her throat. "I want you to know that I'm on your side."

"Thank you," Mrs. Chandler said.

"Men," Mother said.

Silence. I sifted through the accessories, looking for Elaine's gloves. Mother cleared her throat again. "I'm sure you can get back together. For starters, why don't you get Donna at the beauty parlor to do your hair."

One spoon kept stirring. "I'm taking the boys to Florida," Mrs. Chandler said. "To live."

I fastened ermine capes onto Esther and Elaine and hung beaded purses over their arms. Esther gazed at herself in her full-length mirror. "The prince will be there tonight," she said. I leaned closer, thinking their story might begin again, but Elaine still wasn't talking. I twitched her against the table leg, but she stayed quiet.

"Florida?" I heard the silky whisper as my mother crossed her stockinged legs. I knew what she was thinking. President Truman had gone to Florida on vacation and had his picture taken in a short-sleeved, flowered shirt. Florida, as well as Truman, was tacky.

"I can't stay in this town," Mrs. Chandler said.

"Everyone knows," Mother said. There was silence. "But if you fixed yourself up," she continued, "you could fool them."

Esther and Elaine decided to go swimming. Under their dresses, they always wore bathing suits, so I removed the gowns and swam them through the air in an underwater ballet. Crowds gathered to see these glamorous people. The crowds said, "Oooh," and "Ahhh," but I made them whisper, so I could still hear the voices in the next room.

"He's going to marry her," Mrs. Chandler's voice said.

"Oh?" Mother said.

"She's younger," Mrs. Chandler said. "Getting my hair done won't change a thing."

The water ballet ended. Esther and Elaine put on nightgowns and satin slippers. They stood in front of their full-length mirrors and put away their jewels. Esther told Elaine it was important to look beautiful even when they were exhausted.

"I'll find a job," Mrs. Chandler said.

"Work?" Mother asked in a shocked voice. "Your boys need you at home."

Silence.

"Make him support you," Mother said. "That's what is done."

A spoon clattered into the saucer. Someone stood up. Mrs. Chandler said, "I should go home. I have lots of packing to do."

I peeked around and saw them hugging, even though they weren't friends. Mrs. Chandler's eyes still looked like a deer's eyes. It took forever for her to get her arms into the sleeves of her coat. "Sorry I didn't dress up," she said.

"Make him buy you some clothes," Mother said.

After she left, my mother stood a long time by the door, looking out the window. When she went upstairs to change back into Saturday clothes, I wondered what she'd tell Daddy about Mrs. Chandler, a person we didn't even know, coming here. But probably he wasn't supposed to know about it. This had been women's business. As Mother's heels clicked across the upstairs bedroom floor, I packed up the dolls, opening the little tabs on each dress, and tucking everything between the covers of the book.

In my little-girl bedroom, I recall that pink roses twined up the wallpaper behind fuzzy cutouts of Bambi and Thumper. In my closet, clanking hangers held my dresses, and all the shelves behind them were crammed with coloring books, paper dolls, and board games. In my mind, I can walk out my bedroom door, turn right and cross the hall into Mother and Dad's bedroom. In there, it's blue wallpaper, the black Singer sewing machine, and white tie-back curtains at the windows that look out at Amherst Avenue. I remember that Mother kept her hats in boxes, and her shoes tucked into little cloth bags. Her closet was full of secrets. It was where she kept her plans for me.

I imagine that while she waited for me to grow up, she would go to the back of that closet where she might straighten the collar of a jacket or finger-press a pleat. Until I grew into those special clothes, she made my dresses from yards of gingham or dotted Swiss—full-skirted, puffed-sleeved, and sashed.

Each grade school morning, I pulled on my undershirt and panties and slip. Then I chose a dress, passing over the one I hated—there was always one—but rotating the others. After school, as long as I was staying home, I was allowed to dress down, into my flannel shirt and my wonderful dungarees, rolled up to the knees.

When my sixth grade best friend Barbara Turner moved to Long Island, she and I wrote desperate letters planning to visit each other. When summer finally came, I rode the New York Central, feeling grown up, south through Troy and Albany and along the Hudson River to Grand Central Station. Mother saved the note I wrote her.

Dear Mother,

I should have brought my dungarees.

Tuesday Barbara and I rode around on bicycles.

After supper we went to the school and met some boys. It was cool yesterday again and I really needed my dungarees. You can't go around on a bike down here with a dress on.

The girls hardly ever wear dresses down here.

Love, Anne

I can still feel too much air on goose-bumpy legs. I remember over-hearing Mrs. Turner pleading with Barbara to be nice for a couple more days. I can still see Barbara's friends, looking older, looking good, wearing their dungarees.

In 1954, Kurt, the first boy I ever dated who was taller than me, asked me to the Junior Prom. Kurt was a freckle-faced, sweet buffoon, and I was totally in love with him. I imagined we'd be like Cinderella and the prince for one magical, romantic night. "I need a prom dress," I told Mother.

"I have just the thing," she said. The time had finally arrived for the clothes she had stored in the back of her closet. The dress she pulled out was one she'd worn to dances when she was in college. Its dark blue cotton piqué skirt went down to the floor, which made it look grown up. But was it a prom dress?

I told her the other girls were getting their dresses in Glens Falls. I showed her prom dresses in my *American Girl* magazines. She pointed out that this white bolero jacket had flare, and the princess lines of the dress emphasized my slender waist. "Put it on," she said. She pinched it in here and there and shortened the wide shoulder straps. As I practiced walking in my first pair of heels, I tried not to worry.

At the prom, Kurt didn't seem to notice that every other girl was in frothy, pastel tulle with strapless tops held up with bones. Their luscious skirts billowed out to waltz length. I lurked beside the bleachers until we could go home.

A few months later, Dad's transfer to the New York City office was approved. We'd be leaving the small town where I'd lived for sixteen years. In upscale Westchester County, Mother would at last have a place to dress us in the right clothes.

In a photo taken in 1970, my daughters stand side by side on the polished wood stairs. Amy is six, and Rebecca is four. Their red hair is fastened at the crown with elastic bands and ribbons. Their matching blue pinafores are trimmed with black rick rack and big sashes pouf out in back. They're trying with all their might to be good at Grandma's house.

Before we left Oregon, I prepared the girls for the visit. We made lists of things to do there: visit the duck pond by the Parkway, go to the library for books, play on the swings at the grade school. "Keep your voices soft at Grandma Warren's house," I would tell them.

"It's only for a week," I continued, "and then, we'll visit your Smith grandparents where you can be noisy and it won't matter what you wear."

Mother always found fault. "They're spoiled," she said. She advised me to "lay down the law with them." She said, "Why can't you be GOOD girls?" Their faces turned stony, and they turned into delinquents. My quick hugs didn't help. "When we get back home," I told them, "everything will be fine." At least, I was right about that.

Today, the cicadas hush their chatter as I climb the polished stairs where Amy and Rebecca (now grown women) once posed in matching blue pinafores. In the sudden silence, I hear Mother's shoes on her bedroom floor. Her head jerks up as I go in. She's leaning hard on her walker.

Her hair is softly brushed back, her face is perfectly made up. Other than those black, orthopedic shoes, she's naked.

We do the hug anyway.

Twisting a wet slip in her hands, she tells me how her water runs out of her any time at all, how she never knows when it will come, how she is trying to get to the bathroom often, but then she'd gets in there and nothing, but a few minutes later...

"I'm soaking those pads," she says irritably. "I keep soaking those pads, and they're too expensive.

"I've changed clothes too many times today," she continues. "I'm worn out." Her legs wobble and threaten to buckle.

She mustn't fall! I grab a chair and place it behind her. "Sit here," I say, taking her arm, guiding her to step back. She doesn't want to let go of the wet slip. I tug it out of her fingers and toss it into her bathroom sink. I come back with clean panties.

"It's just fine," I say as I hold the panties where she can get her feet into them, "to throw those pads away. That's what they're for." I look up to see if she's listening. She nods, but she tightens her lips in annoyance. I sound extravagant. Or maybe she doesn't like me using a mothering voice with her.

I slide a slip over her head and pull it gently over the grainy age spots on her back. "You just got your hair done. It looks nice."

She nods and sighs. "That was yesterday."

"It looks really nice." She needs a dress now and I turn toward her closet. As the door slides open, I look in, but not too far. This closet still holds polyester plans for me. At least, these days, I'm no longer the only target. There is a daughter-in-law. There are granddaughters.

One December when Amy and Rebecca had grown into college women, we visited Mother and Dad. Sunday morning, Rebecca and I were loading the dishwasher, when Mother came to the top of the stairs.

"I want you up here," she called.

Amy, reading on the couch at the foot of the stairs, must have torn herself away from her page and looked up. "You want me, Grandma?" she asked.

I continued sponging crumbs off the red Formica counters as our French toast breakfast settled heavy in my stomach. I heard closet noises.

"I want the three of you up here."

Three daughters trying to please their mothers, we marched up the stairs. Why was "no" never an option? As we turned into Mother's bedroom, I forced a grin. "Fun," I whispered. My daughters rolled their eyes.

Mother's bedroom no longer held any traces of Dad. He loved to read in the middle of the night, so it was "more convenient" for him to sleep in the other bedroom. This room was all Mother's with rose-and-cream wallpaper and the four-poster cherry bed with the antique bedspread. My wedding photo hung beside the bed—me wearing the wedding dress Mother and the clerk at Lord & Taylor chose for me and the hairdo Mother's hairdresser contrived and sprayed into submission. The girl in that photo has dark circles under her eyes.

Mother stood us in front of the mirror. From her closet she brought out polyester knits, wool jackets, and beaded evening clothes she had worn to DAR conferences. She wanted her clothes out in the world being worn again, but to our eyes, they were dated. Too dressy.

"I was the one with breasts that didn't fit in her clothes," Amy said later. "I'd get stuck in them."

"She desperately needed us to want her things," Rebecca has said. "And why did we have to try everything on?" she asks. "With her watching?"

Mother was sure her clothes would improve us. If we said we had no place to wear the polyester suit with the rhinestone pin, we confirmed her fears about backwater Oregon.

"I'd make up an event where I might wear something just to make her feel good," Rebecca said. "Or to get the whole process over with."

Mother and her closet were too strong for us.

The girls and I, afterwards, pretended we hadn't been jerked around. We told each other none of it mattered.

Mother is cold. "I get to choose a dress for you!" I chirp, fighting my inertia. With great effort I reach into her powerful closet and slide hangers back and forth, sudden tears blurring everything into soft colors. "Think of how much you do now," someone says—I say. "You run this house. You pay the bills. You make sure the yard gets mowed."

Giving power back. Anyone would.

My hands stop on a dress from Lands End, a royal blue knit. I pull it out for her to see, and all at once it's me on the other side of the hanger, desperate for a sale. "This one?"

She stares at the dress, disgusted with my choice.

"No?"

"No!"

The urge to make her try it on shames me. Instead, it occurs to me that certain things will be remembered about this day. I gather up dresses, skirts, and tops and carry them to her. She shakes her head at my exuberance, but then she selects a pin-striped skirt and a lavender pullover.

"You didn't need to get out so many," she says.

After I return her clothes to the closet, I turn around, expecting her to be getting dressed, but with shaking hands, she is smoothing the shirt, turning it over and over in her lap.

I will have to dress her.

Since she's sitting down, I decide to slide the skirt over her head. But her arms are down and the skirt stops like a straight jacket at her shoulders.

"I didn't think that one through," I tell her with a grin. A little smile crosses her face. We start over with her holding her arms up. Then we ease the skirt slowly down until it's reached her hips. She stands a moment so I can pull the waistline zipper closed.

The pullover is next, too tight over her head, threatening to ruin the hairdo. Once it's on, I tuck in the label and untwist the sleeves. Hand over her glasses. "Looking good," I say.

She folds her hands in her lap. "How was your trip?" she asks then. As if I've just now arrived. As if we could erase the last half hour.

"I left home at four this morning." I glance around the bedroom, not sure what else she needs. Everything looks the same in here, including that exhausted bride on the wall. My crimson skirt swirls around my legs as I stand.

I turn back to her, knowing that for a few minutes I held the power. Then, I gave it back. Today I traveled a very long way.

The "Sad Bride" on the author's mother's bedroom wall

Eating for Life

CALYX, A Journal of Art and Literature by Women 28.3 (Summer 2015). Accepted for publication.

SUGAR IN A CUBE

In Ticonderoga, upstate New York, in the 1940s, the war was over; spider plants and geraniums replaced tomatoes in the old Victory Gardens. I was nine.

Summer mornings I would hear a call from the cabinet in our dining room. Wearing my flannel shirt and rolled-up dungarees, I crept through the sleeping house and eased open the cabinet door. My fingers wove through the narrow opening to pluck a sparkling cube from the crystal bowl we used for company.

Minutes later I crossed the field of wild strawberries, climbed high up in the branches of "my" tree. Finally, I placed the cube into my mouth and felt its corners melt into sweet avalanches. Up there in my tree, I dreamed of living somewhere else, a place where people told me my ideas were important. In those places, I no longer wore glasses.

DOG BISCUITS

When I was trapped at the dinner table, Whisky ate whatever I dropped—even the mealy potatoes. He was my best pal, and we decided the two of us were circus bound. With grand gestures, I taught him to sit and roll over and play dead. For the finale, I played a fanfare on my imaginary horn before placing a biscuit on his nose. The audience waited. Whisky stared at the biscuit until his eyes crossed. At last, he flipped it into the air, and caught it in his mouth. What! A! Dog!

Of course, I celebrated with him. Whisky's teeth and mine chewing our biscuits made the same crunchy sounds. Afterwards, our mouths gave off the same dust-bin smell.

Many days, we sat on the porch step, me with my arm around him, him with his silky ear pressed to my cheek. He listened to the stories I told about a dog statue that came to life and carried a girl to darkest India or to the castles on the Rhine. I told him that when my heartbroken real parents came to rescue me, he could come, too.

FLOATING ISLANDS

In seventh grade home economics we hunched over black Singer sewing machines stitching Fifties-style aprons with ruffled bibs and long sashes. Weeks later, we wore our finished aprons to the big kitchen where we made vanilla custard, stirring the mixture of eggs and milk over the burner until it thickened enough to coat a metal spoon. We beat egg whites into soft peaks, added sugar, and mounded fluffy white islands on top of the custard.

We served them in special glasses that our teacher told us were "compotes." Everyone wanted to eat mine because it wasn't scorched. They called me a natural homemaker. I said no. I wasn't.

CHERRY PIE

Mother was the homemaker. She'd gone to the Home Economics College at Cornell and our house was her workshop and kingdom. Everything in the kitchen had a purpose known to her, and each thing was kept in a special place in her crammed cupboards. The brown mixing bowl was only for making cookies; the glass one was only for muffins. Spices were in pretty little jars. Unlabeled. She alone knew which one was cinnamon, which one was allspice.

When Mother left for a National Convention of the Daughters of the American Revolution, I asked Dad if he thought I could make a cherry pie. He said, why not, so I got out Betty Crocker. Since I was in enemy territory, I worked fast. My pie turned out just like the one on the cover of the book. My new friend, Joan, came over for a pie party.

When Mother got home, she said she bet I couldn't do it again. She was right about that. I couldn't. Not with her there.

ARTICHOKES

When Mother asked about my overnight visit to Joan's house, I didn't tell her about the maid or the intercom system or the shiny chrome furniture. "Those people are too different," she would have said, and she would have wrinkled her nose and told me to forget about being friends with Joan.

I wanted to tell her about dinner. How everyone—not just the adults—talked. They discussed art and music and they got me talking. Me! The one who had perfected the silent, intelligent nod. When I told them my dream to become a French interpreter at the UN, they applauded. They said that my first choice, Middlebury College, offered wonderful language programs.

If I told Mother all this, I knew what she'd say. "They were being polite," she would say. "You're going to take home economics just like I did."

She asked again. "Did you like Joan's family?"

I drew a deep, shaky breath. As I answered, she must have been surprised at my angry tone. "They served artichokes," I told her. "I didn't know how to eat mine."

STAND-BY-YOUR-MAN CUISINE

"They'll like you," Fred said as we left the Cornell campus and drove out to his family's farm, "you being in the home economics school and all."

"Mmm," I said and made a mental note not to mention how I lived for my language electives.

Fred's mother Lillie, smiling, with soft curls framing her face, welcomed us in. His dad greeted me with a rough voice and a white forehead—the badge of a man who works in the fields wearing a ball cap. He offered me his hand, washed clean, but lined dark. Lillie slid a roast out of the oven, whisked brown gravy, and told us to sit down.

Potatoes, squash, corn, chutneys, cucumber pickles, yeast rolls, and a cabbage and carrot salad crowded the table. Every fruit and vegetable had been grown and picked and processed there on the farm. Conversation centered on the crops, the weeds, the weather. I nodded intelligently…a lot.

Later over dishwashing, Lillie said, "A farm wife does everything to help her husband." She told me that during harvest she worked long hours to can everything and turn the rest into jams, sauces, purees, and juice. "You can't waste a thing on a farm," she said.

"I'm not right for you," I wailed as Fred and I drove back to campus. "I don't know how to cook a roast."

LIVER AND ONIONS

The wedding cake loomed three tiers tall, but all I really recall about the reception was that I had to talk to people I didn't know. Mother had decided where to hold the wedding and where we would spend the first night of our honeymoon. She chose my dress, my hair, my attendants, the flowers. I couldn't wait to change into the one thing I liked—my navy dress with the cute bolero jacket. I wanted to flee through the shower of rice, drive out of town as a married woman, suddenly free to make my own decisions.

Two weeks later, in our apartment next to the Cornell campus, I leafed through the pages of my new Betty Crocker. What should I fix for our first sit-down dinner at home? Something easy. Something important.

Liver and onions called out to me. Healthy. Conservative. Frugal. Something I didn't really like much.

Something his mother might serve.

RHUBARB

One afternoon we drove out to the farm. In the kitchen, Lillie handed me a knife. "Can you get the rhubarb?" she asked. "We'll have pie tonight."

Strawberries ripened under the hot sun, while cars lined up at the farm stand on the highway. Fred's sister was overseeing the pickers; Fred was in the fields with his dad. In the long rows of the kitchen garden, I pictured myself as the next wife on this farm. I tried to name the vines and leaves and stalks. I couldn't. When I finally chanced upon what had to be rhubarb, I bent toward the plants with relief, my knife ready.

Lillie met me on the back porch, wondering, I'm sure, what had taken so long. "Leaves go in the compost," she said, and taking the knife, she swiftly beheaded each stalk.

"Compost?" I asked. She pointed. When I sighted a pile with other leaves on it, I added mine to it. Would this get easier? Beside me, vines wound their way up strings. A heavy black beetle ran up a vine, fell off, and ran up again.

APPLE WEDGES AND GRAHAM CRACKERS

Graduate student pay at Oklahoma State barely got us to the end of the month. Chicken cost nineteen cents a pound. Pig's feet were even less but Betty Crocker couldn't tell me what to do with pig's feet.

At the college preschool, the source of my paycheck, the head teacher was challenging me to actively teach. I had studied child development at Cornell, she reasoned, surely I could do more than mix paints and serve graham crackers. I forced myself to plan projects, call the children to me. We sang that they were little gray ponies and galloped back to the barn; they flapped their arms like ducklings; they did all the motions to "Where is Thumbkin?" They sat still when I read to them. Maybe, I thought, I could write stories for children.

V-8 JUICE

After a day of collecting duckling imprinting data for the behavioral psychologist, I dragged my pregnant body into our Raleigh apartment. Sagging over the stove, I warmed V-8 in a saucepan and poured it steaming into a tea cup. Sip by sip, eight vegetables slid down my throat and went directly to our baby.

V-8 bolstered my resolutions. Our child would never starve for hugs. Laughter and fun would fill our house. Every dream would be listened to, honored.

Fred dreamed now of being a professor of Ag Economics. He was disappointing his parents; he wouldn't be a farmer, after all. My own dreams surfaced, as well. When this baby got to school, I would teach preschool. I would write picture books, story after story.

GROUND BEEF

When one pound of cheap ground beef was combined with chili powder, canned corn, and tomato paste, and topped with corn bread from the package mix, it turned into "Chili Bake" and lasted all week. Stuffed peppers used only a half pound of the precious beef when it was stretched with bread crumbs, chopped onion, and tomato-rice soup.

Graduate school was behind us, Fred as a new professor at Oregon State didn't earn a lot. I pleated formal drapes for the living room, re-upholstered secondhand furniture, sewed tee shirts and corduroy pants for our daughters. As soon as I had more time I would write those stories.

Somehow that year, money appeared—enough for Fred's backpacking equipment. The day I found out, ground beef spattered in the pan. Seasoned with anger.

JELL-O SALADS

In my kitchen cupboard, packages of lime, lemon, and strawberry Jell-O stood in columns beside cans of mandarin oranges, pineapple chunks, and fruit cocktail. One of the other pre-school moms told me she had more than fifty gelatin molds. She told me her salads sometimes had ten layers going at different angles that formed inner triangles and diamonds. Sometimes, she alternated opaque layers with clear ones. She even made one that went from red to purple, fading through colors like a rainbow. "I love expressing myself this way," she said.

I closed the cupboard door. I had exactly two hours to work on a story about a twelve-year-old whose best friend had stolen her gold locket.

GRANDMA'S FRUITCAKE

After Halloween, I put away my writing. With Fred teaching workshops all over the Pacific Northwest, we were stumbling between being a family of four and a family of three. Holiday traditions, I thought, would surely bring us back into harmony.

The roaster pan held one batch of Grandma's heavy molasses dough heaped with candied fruits, figs, and seeded raisins. With the big wooden spoon, I stirred up four batches to get twelve loaves. I wrapped the baked loaves first in waxed paper and then in silver foil. Some were tucked into boxes to mail back east. The rest stood like silver ingots tied with red ribbons, labeled for friends. Watching those cakes cure and ripen, I wondered if Grandma had ever felt her family slipping away.

CHILI CON CARNE

Before every Christmas we went with neighbors into the Siuslaw National Forest to cut our Christmas trees. That morning started for me, however, in the kitchen chopping onions—ten of them. But I knew how to do onions quickly, slices in one direction, cubes in the other. With a freshly sharpened knife, my tears didn't start until onion number three.

The onions simmered with chopped green peppers and ground beef before I added beans, stewed tomatoes, and spices—chili powder, cumin, oregano, cayenne, thyme, and garlic. Once it was cooked, the crock pot kept it hot for hours.

With our trees lashed to the top of the Scout, we drove the wet highway back into town, returning to a house rich with chili smells. The fire blazed in the fireplace, and the neighbors reappeared with beer enough for an army. We ate chili while our jackets and mittens and hats dried in the basement. Out on the deck, the freshly cut tree shone beautiful in the rain. Our family silences and misunderstandings wafted up the chimney with the smoke; Fred would be home with us for the rest of the month.

TIDBITS AND CANAPES

In early December, New Year's Eve invitations went out to friends, parents of our children's friends, neighbors, the book group, the knitting group, and the gourmet group.

On December 31st the kitchen windows steamed over as I baked loaves of sweet breads. The refrigerator filled up with cheese spreads and crab dips. I rolled a cheese ball in chopped nuts, and filled the chafing dish with Vienna sausages, teriyaki meatballs, and pineapple chunks. I sewed my dress, a royal blue satin sheath topped by a chiffon tent dress with a skirt that belled around my knees. When I stepped into four-inch heels and put on blue rhinestones, my daughters said I looked like a movie star.

Our friends danced to Bob Marley in the family room. Candles glowed all over the house, and silver garlands shimmered across the mantel.

Fred and I leaned against each other, in love with the way we could throw a good party. No longer an Ag Economist, he worked now for Sea Grant, consulting every place there was a fishing industry—Alaska, California, Mexico, even Chile. Our calendar for the new year was already dark with notes of his leaving.

MOTHER'S OVEN-BAKED CHICKEN

I called her on the phone to ask.

"Well, yes," she said. "You start with a package of chicken parts."

"Didn't I see you melt margarine in the bottom of the pan? How much?"

"A stick," she said. "I guess."

"Aren't there bread crumbs? Spices? What spices do you use?"

"Oh, this and that," she said.

If I told her I was carrying this family alone, what advice would she give me?

SOOT

In early spring at Willamette Park, my Campfire Girls—the twelve fifth-graders who called me "Mom"—rolled ground beef into little balls. They cut potatoes, carrots, and onions into cubes. We sealed the food into foil packages and nestled them into the coals.

While they cooked, we twisted dough around green sticks and toasted them over the flames. The stick left a perfect hole for squirting in jam. Everything we ate was garnished with delicious black specks.

GREEN PEPPERS

Our up-the-street neighbors invited us to dinner. While the others chatted in the living room, I offered to help Ben with the salad.

He rubbed garlic into the wooden bowl and then sipped from his glass of Scotch. "Tell me what you're writing," he said.

"Short stories for kids. I work at the dining room table. Keep getting interrupted." My fingers itched to get going on the salad; mine were always made before company came. He rinsed and dried a green pepper. As I reached for it to cut quick slices, he stopped me. "Have you ever noticed," he asked, "how beautiful a green pepper is?"

Many of the paintings hanging in this house were his. I stared at the pepper as if I, too, were an artist—noticing the waxy sheen of skin, the dusky pigment underneath.

When I looked up he was smiling at me. "You need a better place to write," he said. "A place that is yours."

Sudden tears burned my eyes.

With gentle fingers he took the knife from me and sliced the pepper himself.

FAST FOOD

From my kitchen window I could see the other husbands coming home. They came by car; they biked; they walked. For a change, mine would be coming, too. He had been in northern California most of last week and would leave for Washington, DC, on Thursday. His favorite dinner was in the oven—baked chicken, sweet potatoes.

I dawdled at the sink and looked again out the window. There! There was the husband I was watching for. He was careful not to look at my window as he pedaled up the hill to his own house, his own wife. Lately, my conversations with Ben had become too intimate; we understood each other's dreams, his painting, my writing, too well. Guilt had taken up residence in my home, along with sadness and terror.

My husband wheeled into the driveway.

In quick time, I ripped lettuce, sliced tomatoes, red onion, cucumbers. All efficiency, I slid the salad onto the table along with the place mats, silverware, a couple of hot pads for the baked dishes. A bouquet of sweet daphne in the center. I forked steaming chicken onto the platter, called the girls.

FIRE EXTINGUISHER GARNISH

"It was on fire," Fred said. "I had to do something."

I peered into the oven at what had been a perfectly good meatloaf. I'd only been gone an hour...

He could tell I was mad and was already backing out of the kitchen. "How come you went off and left it?" he asked.

"How come you didn't just throw baking soda onto the oven floor," I answered. "That's where the fire was."

He turned away. Home was his place to be calm, to rest up before the next trip. I never greeted him with full garbage cans or leaky faucets. I thawed frozen pipes with the hair dryer, taught the girls to drive, got to know their boyfriends.

"I had everything timed so I could run a thousand errands and there would still be dinner before the game." I slammed the oven door closed. "You ruined it," I yelled. "YOU fix it."

Silence filled the kitchen as we both remembered that he didn't know how. I could sense the girls in their bedrooms, holding their breath and listening to parents who had fallen out of love. Just as I had listened when I was little.

THE LAST CHRISTMAS DINNER

As usual, we would have chicken with dumplings, sweet potatoes, and cherry pie. In the next room our own tree held ornaments we had made over the last twenty-five years—family memories that, next week, I would pack away forever. This was the last year we would bake gingerbread girls and boys and decorate them in bikinis and overalls. The last year of driving into the rainy forest to cut our tree while chili steamed in the crock pot.

I minced onion extra fine while Mother and I wasted kitchen moments in small talk. She and Dad didn't know I had started divorce proceedings. No matter how Fred and I agonized and plotted, neither of us could figure out how to tell them.

THE NEXT THANKSGIVING

Amy, now a college student, came from her apartment in Portland, seemingly unfazed by the idea of a different kind of Thanksgiving.

"Remember how it was," I asked her as we sat down at the restaurant, "with twenty people around the table, half of them graduate students?"

"Mostly from other countries," she said. "Everyone brought something strange to go with the turkey."

"Fish-eye pudding from Thailand."

"Curried rice with sea weed."

"Your dad," I said, "always gave a lecture about the first Thanksgiving." We grinned, remembering how annoying that was. "But his students were interested. Afterwards," I paused to sigh, "goblets and wine glasses to wash by hand. Cranberry stains in the linen napkins. Gravy on the big cloth. Load after load of plates in the dishwasher."

The waiter came to our table, flourishing the special Thanksgiving menu.

"I'll have prime rib," I told him.

"Salmon for me," Amy said.

BUDGET GOURMET

I scrambled to earn money to supplement the royalties from my children's books. I taught writing at the community college, worked as a technical editor at an engineering firm, and signed on as a publicist for the music department on the OSU campus. Three part-time jobs, plus writing a book. Microwave dinners were the cuisine of the day.

Mother's letters, which arrived each week, contained two themes: (1) Divorce had ruined my life, and (2) I was a terrible example for my daughters. "I stuck it out," she wrote. "You should have done that, too." Eventually, I stopped opening her letters.

After dinner of three-cheese lasagna, I snuggled into the couch with student papers. Classical music played on the stereo. The girls were both in college. For the first time in my life, I had only myself to please.

CREAMED MUSHROOMS ON TOAST

My longtime friend Jerry, a potter, dropped by to tell me his wife had left him. He wasn't going to stay for supper, but we kept on talking, and the mushrooms were the only decent thing in the refrigerator.

"I don't date recently divorced men," I had told everyone. "They whine a lot. They only want someone to rescue them from the laundry."

This one seemed different.

We talked about how potters and writers work in similar ways to turn raw material into art. We talked about needing space and time to be alone. He said he admired the way I had taken charge of my life.

He asked for seconds.

CORN ON THE COB

In upstate New York in August, I carried the bag of corn into Mother's kitchen. As the cobs thumped out on the red Formica counter, I remembered long-ago August days when Dad would tell Mother to start the water boiling. "Five minutes from the field to the kettle," he'd say. "That's the way to do it." He'd grin all the way to the farmer's stand and back.

Mother pounded her walker into the kitchen. These hot days swelled her ankles into bulges. "Put that paper bag in the bottom of the sink," she said.

I peeled the husk from the first ear and golden kernels emerged.

"Put this in the sink." She grabbed the bag and rattled it at me. In her voice was the knowledge that I had never stopped being a disappointment to her.

I set down the first ear and considered the others. Part of me wanted to run like Forrest Gump back to Oregon and Jerry. Part of me remembered that her ninety-year-old fingers weren't up to husking corn, and my sixty-five-year-old fingers were. And it was her kitchen. Her sink.

But why did this mother stay so angry? We were two women, growing older. Dad was dying, growing weaker each time I visited. Weren't there things we should be saying?

I was visiting them every other month. Before each trip I fortified myself with positive thinking and lists of things to fill the time. I had even practiced meditation hums. "Hmmmm," I said now, surprised and delighted at the power of one hum.

I pushed the bag into the bottom of the sink and husked the corn the way she told me. Each ear deserved a hum, and each ear got one. Finally, I folded up the corners and plastic-bagged the bundle.

"Use two plastic bags," she said. "They leak."

By this time next week, I would be back in my own kitchen. I would buy Oregon sweet corn and while I husked it, I would remember Dad back when he was young and strong, grinning through the doorway, telling us to start the water.

ALGAE

Rebecca drove to Corvallis for a visit. As I started to pour her a glass of water, she stopped me. "Mom," she said, her voice shocked. She held the Britta pitcher up to the window, and we could see green "things" swaying inside. For heaven's sakes!

"I'm not the homemaker of old," I said.

TODAY'S STIR-FRY

Around four o'clock I left my desk to check the thawing chicken breast. It was still slightly frozen, so I cut it into paper thin slices, added olive oil, soy sauce, chopped ginger and garlic. Closer to dinner time, Jerry started the rice. We got out the cribbage board and cut for the deal.

Jerry was the wok man at our house and, shortly before the rice was finished, he fired up the gas burner and sautéed the marinated chicken. Garlic and ginger smells filled the kitchen. Broccoli crowns turned emerald green. A few minutes later, we dished everything into pottery boats, ones he had made, perfect for this beautiful meal.

WONDER BREAD

I was swimming three days a week, teaching a class, walking two miles, biking, working out at the gym. Fit. Busy. A new book coming out.

Too busy to get ovarian cancer.

As people do, we tried to make sense of this.

Was it those sugar lumps I stole as a child? Was it the result of living with parents who were emotionally cold? My fear of failing as a farm wife, and later as a faculty wife? The fatty ground beef I bought in the Six-ties to make the 365 recipes in that cookbook? The campfire soot? The trauma of ending my marriage?

Eleven days after my first chemo, when my im-mune system was most compromised, I had emergency surgery to remove a bowel obstruction. Jerry, fighting to keep the worry from his face, bent over the gurney to tell me he loved me. We had loved for twenty sweet years.

After that surgery, my instructions were to keep doing chemo and also gain back fifteen pounds while eating no seeds, nuts, black pepper or whole spices, and nothing made of whole wheat or brown rice. No raw fruits or vegetables. My new menu was completely out of whack with what we usually ate.

Lauri brought rich croissants from Le Patisserie. Lynn brought nutless fudge. Jan's apple pie had a crust formed of little pastry apples. Carlien appeared with creme brulée—cup after cup. And then, she made soup that tasted wonderful in spite of no onions, no celery, no spices. Rebecca made a strained "Miracle Broth," composed of twenty vegetables and seaweed. Jerry slid easy-over eggs onto soft white bread.

CHAMPAGNE

Nine months went by. After several chemo sessions plus another surgery to remove tumors, my numbers dropped to normal. "Normal" lasted one year. We got out the champagne glasses to celebrate.

The odds were not good. Eighty percent of us recur.

Three months later, I did.

DOLLOPS OF ADVICE

Drink green tea four times a day. Never microwave the bag. Take baby aspirin. No, it's too late for baby asprin. Turmeric stops cancer. Eat nothing that is white. Drink energized water, but is the $5000 filter system worth it? Meditate. Avoid refined sugars. Avoid meat. Order a special juice from Tahiti. Listen to music. Make that miracle broth. Take vitamin C. Avoid vitamin C. Bring flowers into the house.

My doctors, on the other hand, tell me I may eat anything in the world that I enjoy.

Three years to live is my new norm, but I know women whose remissions have lasted longer. Why not me?

I add "hope" to my list of ingredients.

The author's brother (Jack Warren) and the author

About the Author

Anne Warren Smith started writing as a child—a saga about a girl—herself—who climbed on the back of a magic statue—a large dog—and traveled the world having fantastic adventures. Only at night, of course, and always home in time for breakfast. She also taught as a child—to lines of dolls in front of a chalky blackboard.

Since the Seventies, she has written ten books, six of which are published, plus a number of unpublished picture books. When feeling more "grown up," Anne writes memoir—essays about her family, essays about life, and several of those are published in literary journals and online on the *Christian Science Monitor* home page. Her mother always wanted her to be published in *Reader's Digest*, but she failed at this.

The writing classroom has drawn her for more than twenty-five years, mostly at the Benton Center in Corvallis. Other classrooms and workshops were at conferences sponsored by the Society of Children's Writers and Illustrators, Pacific Northwest Writer's Association based in Seattle, and Willamette Writers based in Portland. She loves working with other writers, helping them whenever possible to grow. She believes that writing for publication is mostly accomplished by perseverance, saying, "In my opinion, talent is nice, but not as important as the bulldog approach."

Hundreds of printed rejections have entered her postal mailbox and more rejection notes have flowed into her computer inbox. Somewhere in her office, is a thick file of printed rejections, "Why on earth have I saved them? I don't know," she wonders.

Good writing years have followed bad ones. Anne has written hundreds of pieces that didn't quite work. She has sent out pieces before they were ready. When several publishing houses consolidated; one of her editors was fired and the book that had been accepted came back. She has hired and fired two agents, negotiated her own contracts, and despaired of finding time to write while holding down other jobs.

In 2012 Anne's ovarian cancer returned for the last time after fifteen months of remission. She continued to enjoy her life fully, casting a shadow of her own shape, going her own way, like tulips, and loving deeply and well. In 2015, as she entered into hospice care, Anne and her "Writing Muses" (Lynn and Mary), decided to create this collection of published and unpublished essays. In spite of uncertainties about the future, life is always beginning again and is full of hope, good stories, and lots of love.

Read Anne's blog, "Write for Your Life!" at https://annewarrensmith.wordpress.com/